Revolution and International Politics

Revolution and International Politics

Peter Calvert

Professor of Comparative and International Politics, University of Southampton

St. Martin's Press, New York

Library of Congress Cataloging in Publication Data
Calvert, Peter.
    Revolution and international politics.
    1. Revolutions.   2. International relations.
I. Title.
JC491.C235 1983   327.1   83-9640
ISBN 0-312-67985-8

Contents

1 The analysis of revolution

The purpose of this book is to explore the nature of revolution in the context of international politics and, by doing so, to cast new light on the nature of international politics today. 'International politics' is here seen as comprising not only the formal relations between states, the main focus of the sub-discipline commonly known as 'international relations', but also all interactions across formally constituted state boundaries. It is the peculiar characteristic of revolution, as that term is commonly used today, that it not only affects the politics of individual states, but seeks to change those of others, and even to call into question the very nature of state boundaries and of the international system of which they have for so long been an essential part.

But what is revolution? Despite the intense interest that the subject has attracted in both scholarly and popular literature over the past twenty years, it remains as elusive as ever. In my study of the concept of revolution (Calvert 1970a) I traced the history of the concept from its origin in the times of the Italian Renaissance. Then it meant a sudden seizure of state power or the forcible overthrow of a ruler. Today we would call this a coup, and that is the term that will be used here. But it is from these origins that the root meaning of the term 'revolution' comes, and for this reason the idea of violence, real or threatened, is inseparable from it. Since the French Revolution in 1789, however, the word 'revolution' has more specifically come to mean a major change in the political and socio-economic structure of an individual state, brought about by the spontaneous efforts of its citizens, though these efforts may be aided from outside and may in turn act to bring about similar changes in other countries (see *inter alia* Johnson 1964, Moore 1969, Eisenstadt 1978, Skocpol 1979, Billington 1980).

In this book, therefore, I propose to make use of a broad definition of revolution which will comprehend a wide range of phenomena. What these have in common is the forcible overthrow of a government or regime. For many social scientists such an overthrow is not a revolution unless it is attended or directly followed by far-reaching social or economic transformation of the country concerned. For the student of politics, however, and more particularly for the practitioner of international relations, for whom this book is intended, the problem is that in the modern world there are now very many movements and individuals claiming the proud title of revolutionary. Many of these will justify their seizure of power by the fact that they are revolutionaries, that they intend, that is to say, to carry out such profound transformations that their seizure of power is thereby justified. Yet very few such transformations take place even now, and the result is that the observer of revolution is presented with a unique conceptual problem: how is he to know what to study when, in effect, a revolution is defined not by its origins or events, but by its consequences?

The only possible approach which promises success, therefore, is to adopt a broad definition, and to treat all such seizures of power or depositions as revolutions, at least until proved otherwise. But this approach also has positive benefits. It draws our attention to the great similarities that all such movements have with one another. It emphasises the close relationship between, for example, social revolution on the one hand, and pre-emptive military coups on the other. It enables us to study problems on a small scale, such as diplomatic recognition and armed intervention, which in the scale of a major social transformation can lead, and have in the past led, to huge conflicts of global proportions, and which cannot safely be permitted to do so in the future without running the risk of the total annihilation of humanity— an extreme form of what Marx termed 'the common ruin of the contending parties'.

First of all, then, we need a framework for the analysis of revolution. Revolution can be viewed in four different ways (Calvert 1970b). Firstly, revolution is a process by which people become disenchanted with the incumbent government, on which they focus their failure to attain their political demands. Secondly, it is an event in which an existing government is overthrown and a new one established in its place. Thirdly, it is a program of change instituted and carried through by the incoming government. Lastly, it is a myth, describing the sequence of events in terms which serve to legitimise the actions of the incoming government and the program it has instituted.

The common factor here is the event, and it is therefore with the event that we must begin. The fall of a government is the determining feature without which a revolution cannot be deemed to have taken place. It is not, however, the only feature of interest. Like all other historical events, revolutionary events (as I shall call them to distinguish them from the general phenomenon of revolution) are preceded by causes and followed by consequences. And all but the simplest events may be difficult to unravel in terms of their causes precisely because of the element of surprise that so often attends their onset. Yet it is certainly not true that such events are wholly spontaneous. The use of force to bring about political (and by extension social) change is something that, to be successful, demands an element of preparation, and if interesting consequences are to follow, then, after the event, the new government will have to consolidate its own hold on power. Hence I propose to follow D. J. Goodspeed (Goodspeed 1962), and divide revolutions, coups, etc., into three stages: preparation, action and consolidation.

The sequence of preparation, action and consolidation obviously is a meaningful way of looking at a military action, in so far as revolutions are military actions. Revolutions are, of course, in many other respects not military but political actions, but this does not invalidate the approach. After all, to take a parallel from non-violent politics, one does not go into a general election without preparing for it, or, more accurately, if like the British Labour Party in 1983 one does go into a general election without preparing for it then one does not win. The event of the general election (the actual process of choice) is complete when the votes are counted, but the formation of a government is something that necessarily takes some time, and creation of a change in policy is something that one does not expect to be visible overnight. So, too, in revolutions one finds after the event a period of consolidation which we shall discuss in more detail later, which incorporates at least two major elements—one, the actions taken by the government to ensure its own immediate survival, and two, the introduction of a program of new policy or policies, designed to carry out the objectives of the revolutionary movement.

In strategic terms, it is possible to think of the action phase as being sub-divided into three main varieties: the coup; urban insurrection; and guerrilla warfare. We are concerned first with the preparation for all three of these—all those kinds of activities that people go through before any of these types of action begin. But we will be concerned in the first instance with the coup, because, firstly, the coup is very much more frequent than the other types of revolutionary activity and also the prevalent form in our own time; and secondly, it is a small-scale action compared with the relatively spontaneous unplanned urban insurrection, or the long-term campaign associated with guerrilla warfare. It is something that can be studied in some detail in miniature. Therefore we can expect that the information that we derive from this will be of value to the other two cases, whereas it may be hard in the other two cases to disentangle the relevant from the irrelevant. I shall therefore use examples drawn from the coup to illustrate the problems of the preparation phase.

PREPARATION

First of all, we have to think about the question of objectives. Revolutionaries must have, if they are to be successful, clear and relevant strategic objectives; clear, because obviously they have to know what they are doing and, in the case of anything going wrong, they may be in considerable personal danger; relevant, because if they do not seek an effective political target and destroy it, they are going to fail in their overall objective, and they are then going to be very much at risk. Goodspeed gives the very interesting example of Dublin in 1916, where the revolutionaries sought to liberate Ireland by capturing Dublin and by proclaiming the Irish Republic.

They believed that this would be the central element in a vast nationwide uprising. Unfortunately, owing to internal doubts and dissensions they cancelled their plans for the nation-wide uprising a week or two before the actual attempt. What happened therefore was a rising in Dublin itself. But Dublin was not, although the capital of Ireland, the actual centre of power in Ireland. As Goodspeed is at pains to point out, the actual centre of military power in Ireland was in fact in England, as the reserve of military force available in the rest of the United Kingdom was such that the capture of political power in Dublin itself was not sufficient.

Secondly, in their seizure of Dublin, the revolutionaries made a major strategic blunder in that they failed to seize Dublin Castle which was the symbolic centre of power. They believed that the Castle would be impregnable, though in fact such was the scarcity of military manpower in 1916 that only one elderly nightwatchman was on duty at the time. Instead they concentrated on the Post Office which, as the centre of communications was very important, but as a military centre was negligible.

Thirdly, revolutionaries need accurate information. If they are going to form strategic objectives they have not only got to be clear about what they are going to do and to embark upon relevant objectives in military and political terms, they have to be accurate in their assessment of the situation.

In the October Revolution in Russia, it was Lenin's aware-ness of the fact that the government was extremely weak that led him in the end to throw in his support with those who believed in the immediate seizure of power. Whereas many of his supporters were inclined on theoretical grounds to assume that the government was much stronger than it actually was, he correctly recognised that it was not, and therefore was prepared to revise his theoretical notions in the light of the actualities that confronted him. Similarly, the French government of 1789—widely held to be the strongest in Europe and normally recognised as being such, was in fact very weak, although its downfall resulted more from accident rather than from pre-planning. The kind of spontaneous urban insurrection which was characteristic of the French Revolution has therefore never satisfactorily been repeated in any other country. The lack of plan, and the lack of organisation, would not be practicable in the modern state that had the lessons of the French Revolution before it, and in fact even in France it has not been duplicated in precisely the same way.

To turn to the tactical level, the initial problem is one of objectives. The first of these is the 'neutralisation' of government. 'Neutralisation' is a fashionable euphemism nowadays which usually means killing people. If used in its correct sense, that is 'to render the government ineffective', then this certainly is all that the revolutionary need actually do. It is not necessary for him to kill all the members of the incumbent government, and in fact members of incumbent governments do show a startling capacity for survival under most possible circumstances. The reason is that people are politically effective only in so far as they actually play the role that is assigned to them. In Russia in 1917, Kerensky and his government, although they held the title of ministers and were carrying on the functions of ministers, were not in fact 'connected up' to the rest of Russia in such a way that they could actually be effective rulers. Therefore their overthrow did not require or in fact involve their physical destruction.

The reason why the individuals who comprise the government are not necessarily meaningful in any individual sense and what matters is their role in relation to the governmental machine, is that the maintenance of the governmental machine involves the support of the police, of the military and (if separate) of the intelligence forces. The major target of all revolutionary actions, whether coups, urban insurrections or even guerrilla wars, tends to be the communications network, and in an urban context, one finds the centres of communications, the television stations, radio stations, means of transport, on which the military concentrate, are in fact ways in which government communicate with the supporting forces. Hence they are precisely the targets which are selected first for attack by the military or by anyone else.

What it basically comes down to is a question of targets. The seizure of political power, even in this 'century of revolutions' (cf. Gross 1958) is not a straightforward business at all, and it is not even particularly straightforward for the military who do it more often than anybody else. There is a real difficulty in selecting optimal targets, because, as we have already noted, a coup or revolution is not simply a military activity it is also a political one. It is possible, for example, for a hostile force, an opposition, like any foreign power might, to disrupt the functioning of the state, for example by the sabotage of communications. And some revolutionaries have been carried away into believing that these kinds of acts of disruption, sabotage and even sporadic terrorism can actually bring about political changes of major significance. What in practice tends to happen is exactly the reverse; that in fact any attempt to do this kind of thing results in increased support for the government and governmental leaders who, even if first-rank communications are disrupted, usually have at their disposal a substantial layer of second-rank communications.

Every major power that has had to face up to the possibility of war (and what power in the past century has not had to face up to such possibilities at one time or another?) has not only got a very sophisticated first-line defence capacity which, of course, includes its own communications, but also a sophisticated second-line defence capacity. Take first the case of communications. National medium- and long-wave radio stations are now backed up by a chain of FM stations, backed up by local radio stations, backed up in turn, if necessary, by amateur radio stations. The sabotage of a major central telephone exchange in the 1930s no doubt would have disrupted telephone communications almost completely. Today, with automatic exchanges, radio relays and satellites this just is not practicable. Sabotage on this scale is no longer possible in the sophisticated modern state. It may still be meaningful in the more unsophisticated Third World states. Where this is so, however, the second rank of communications is normally entirely in military hands anyway. Hence the military can step in at any time, using their reserve communications systems, disrupt the official communications, outflank the government and seize political power, should they have the wish to do so.

A distinction can be made, moreover, between symbolic

and actual values in targets. The government may not hold any real power, like Kerensky's government in 1917, but it is not sufficient for revolutionaries to disregard it. Governments have a symbolic meaning and revolutionaries who seek to seize political power therefore have always had to grapple with the fact that they cannot simply pretend the government is not there and hope that it will go away. Nor, conversely, can they assume that their view of the real centres of political power in a country are shared by the inhabitants at large; that as symbolic centres of power there are symbolic gestures that have to be made; there are symbolic roles to be played as well as actual ones.

Next comes the question of contingency planning. All standard military theory assumes the existence of contingency planning, that a general can change his mind in the course of military operation. Ever since the Schlieffen Plan went into action in August 1914 and it proved impossible to reverse, once it was actually started, all military strategists have been much more acutely aware of the existence of a need for contingency planning, allowing for tactical changes in the course of the strategically-planned operation (Holsti 1967, pp. 358–61).

But there are very different problems here for the revolutionary. Luttwak (1968), for example, assumes that leaders should not take part in a military coup, that they should be outside, exercising a directing role and prepared to go to the radio station in time to make the appropriate broadcast announcing that they have taken over political power. This is all very well as theory but it does not fit the observed facts. I find it extremely hard to believe that members of most military forces would be seen gallantly storming the barricades on behalf of a set of leaders who were not actually present. Goodspeed more accurately, I think, assesses the highly symbolic importance of leaders' actions in leading their forces, but at the same time he recognises that to do this is to take them out of communication with the rest of their troops; that if a change of plan has to be made all kinds of disastrous consequences may follow. Unlike regular military operations a revolution is not a legal activity, therefore leaders cannot expect that if they are going into this sort of thing they can change their minds in the middle without some risk of disaster. Contingency planning may not be needed in well-planned military coups. But there are far more military coups every year that fail than actually succeed, contrary to popular belief, and when we hear for example, as we frequently do, that, say, Bolivia is a country which has had 185 military coups in the course of its century and a half of independence, we could easily forget that most of these military coups were unsuccessful.

It cannot be assumed even by the military that they can successfully take over political power without someone realising what they are doing and trying to stop them. And it is an observation repeatedly confirmed by experience that it almost invariably seems to be known by a government beforehand that a military coup is under preparation; and the only difference between countries in which military coups are successful, and countries in which they are unsuccessful seems to be that in the former there are so many military coups going on at any given moment, that a government cannot possibly plan to anticipate all of them.

Occasionally one gets a haphazard situation, as in the 1974 seizure of political power in Bolivia itself, where there were two coups going on at the same time—a right-wing one and a left-wing one. Because of this the government had to fight in one direction and then turn round and fight in the other direction. In fact what happened in this particular case was that, no sooner had the government been overthrown, than the successor government was in turn overthrown. It took only about twenty-four hours, but the whole point of it would be missed if one did not realise that there were two actions going on simultaneously. It also made the outcome particularly bloodthirsty—usually military coups are rather mild in terms of casualties.

And the last point is that even at the level of the coup one has to be aware of the problems of preparation that are much wider than the military aspect; that when the military set about preparing a coup they have to carry out certain kinds of political activities as well; they have to engage in negotiations—what Finer calls the *trabajos* ('works')—and they have to make bargains—which Finer calls the *compromisos* (Finer 1962).

The thing about such agreements is that, being completely illegal, they are not always adhered to. One of the joys of bargaining in such a bargaining situation is that it is often the case that someone feels they have been swindled. This, in due course, gives fertile ground for the next military coup, in a couple of years' time. Which is one of the reasons why when countries start having military coups they go on, because in a situation in which no one can trust anyone else, in which all bargaining is conditional, then very rapidly the foundations of political stability are altogether eroded. Stability in the political system is based on the assurance that if you do X then Y will result. If you pay your taxes and are a loyal citizen you will receive social security when you are out of work.

There are, however, two other problems of the coup which are also problems of all other forms of revolutionary activity. First of all, the seizure of political power almost inevitably involves direct physical control of the capital area as such, or at least of the members of the government. It is impossible for a government to look convincingly as if it was in control of its country, unless it controls the national capital. It is the centre of communications, the diplomatic centre, the focus of symbolic loyalties for the whole nation. There is virtually an unwritten rule that unless it holds the capital, a government is not properly the government of the country. But this, of course, in itself raises a question: what are the links between the seizure of political power in the capital and command in the provinces? So often we read of military coups where General X has seized the person of the president of the republic and sent him into exile, and now he, the Commander-in-Chief of the forces, has assumed political power, and we wonder how it is that his authority is then going to hold in the outer provinces? He may have seized power in the capital, but how can this mean that he actually has political power in the country as a whole?

Now there are two possible answers to this: first of all, there is a general assumption in most countries that the orders which have come from the government in the capital are to be followed in default of any others. This is easier to do if orders do not come from the capital very often anyway. Hence, if the country is fairly loose and decentralised, and the capital does not exercise a great deal of political control, if, in short, you do not pay very much in the way of taxes to the capital and you do not get very much in return, then there is no particular incentive one way or another to worry very much about what happens in the capital. In other words, you begin to adopt a philosophical attitude towards coups, revolutions and uprisings of all sorts.

The second point is that the most well-connected aspect of the coup is either the pre-determined bargains, or the hastily-reached agreements with provincial leaders as to which government they are going to support. Sometimes provincial leaders are involved in the compromises taking place before the event, but more often they seem to be arrived at after political power has actually been seized and there is a distinct difference here between one kind of military coup and another—the kind of uprising in which leaders seize political power and then wait for provincial centres to agree or disagree with their decision.

In the latter case, if they disagree, they will be suppressed. Alternatively, there are occasionally provincial uprisings. There are even certain states in which there is not one centre of political power—there are two or more. A very good example is Ecuador, where the capital Quito has always been subjected to intense rivalry from the port city of Guayaquil, which is a very powerful centre of economic power. Whatever the Quiteños do, the people of Guayaquil do not like anyway, so that frequently you find that the sign of the downfall of a government in Ecuador is a revolt in the rival centre. The military will then 'pronounce' against the government and later the commanders in the capital decide whether they are going to support this revolt or not.

The last question concerns the government's links with the larger international system, with foreign support. All governments exist in an international environment and governments coming to power suddenly are not automatically recognised by the international community. Most countries, all other things being equal, recognise new governments on the grounds that they are effectively in control of the country. But often there are considerable ideological reservations against recognition and even where, for example, the present government of Chile has been in control of the state since 1973, it is still not recognised by the Soviet Union. Similarly, in 1903, Britain refused to recognise the government that came to power as a result of the murder of the King of Serbia. The Americans have also used the device of non-recognition, to try and force political bargains on other countries, especially in the case of Mexico and the Caribbean. However, this is unpopular nowadays with countries who like to feel that they can establish their own politics in whatever way they like, without the great powers interfering with them. Hence it is only with a really outrageous case such as Chile or Greece that everyone can exercise that capacity for being sanctimonious which is so strong in human nature and express their disapproval by non-recognition. The Provisional Government of Nicaragua was recognised by the United States in 1979, and has retained that recognition ever since. This suggests that the foreign linkage is mostly not particularly important from the point of view of actual survival, and this is because in most cases governments are overthrown by military movements and the military are, of course, already armed and prepared by their own governments.

In the case of a civilian movement, the question of foreign support would become very much more important; and in guerrilla war, for example, there is an ambiguous moment at the introduction of a guerrilla movement to a provincial area in which it probably has to rely on external support of some kind. Thus, Che Guevara's expedition to Bolivia arrived with everything needed for insurrection. They then proceeded to hide it all under a rock where it was simply dug up by Bolivian government forces—complete indeed with photographs of every member of the group. (It seems unlikely that there could ever have been a revolutionary movement in which people spent so much of their time photographing each other.) The evidence of linkage with foreign groups enabled the Bolivians to present the expedition as being a foreign attempt at subversion, which weakened the basis of its claim to be of Bolivian origin and ancestry. So connections with foreign groups, in other words, present not only the problem of security which any other question of bargaining or appeal making presents, but also that of whether its leaders can appear to be taking part in an anti-national movement or not.

Governments, on the other hand, have a perfect right to carry on negotiations with any foreign country they wish. If the government of Brazil, for example, feels that it is faced with the prospect of subversion, it is perfectly in order for it to go to the United States and buy all the helicopters it needs for counter-insurgency work. It is a legitimate function of any established government to do this. It is therefore a recognised feature of the international system that it is stacked in favour of incumbent governments. And therefore any attempt at negotiation with foreign powers by insurgents necessarily endangers the success of a revolutionary movement in that leakage of information is all too likely in a foreign capital, where people do not have the same interest in security that people at home have. On the other hand, as we shall see, foreign aid and intervention are of very great significance in the later stages of revolution, if a movement is stalled, or where the effect of a change of power in an individual country crucially threatens the stability of the structure of contending alliances.

ACTION

The reason that the coup, guerrilla warfare and urban insurrection form the three main forms of revolutionary action stems from the fact, already mentioned above, that the centres of political power are focused on the government and on the national capital. The overthrow of a government can, therefore, be achieved by action on four distinct levels: the executive power holder, the government, the capital or the province (Calvert 1967, 1970b). It does not, of course, follow that in any given instance any one of these forms is practicable, still less more than one.

The minimal case is that of an attack on the executive power holder, almost invariably in the form of political assassination. Many writers do not like to think of political assassination as a form of 'revolution' because it is not a seizure of political power, merely the removal of an incumbent government. But it has been studied (Leiden and Schmitt 1968, Kirkham *et al.* 1970) in the same context, to which it is clearly related, and hence it does tell us something about the strategy of political violence.

It has been well recognised since at least the time of Machiavelli (Machiavelli 1950) that, in the last analysis, it is not possible to defend a head of state or head of government against political assassination, if the assassin is not backed by an organised movement, and there is practically no chance therefore of him giving away his intentions in advance. But in practice, self-betrayal is quite common, and the more so because most, if not all, assassinations of prominent political figures have a clear political motive. It appears, for example, that all the assassinations of American Presidents were politically motivated. With the possible exception of Lee Harvey Oswald, the background of each of the assassins is such that the idea that the assassinations of Presidents are exactly like any other kind of murder, is obviously wrong in that all these people have some kind of strong political motivation. John Wilkes Booth, for example, was pro-southerner and shot Lincoln out of a sense of revenge for the Civil War; Garfield was shot by a disappointed office-seeker and McKinley was shot down by an acknowledged anarchist, who announced that he was doing it for anarchist reasons.

We can even go so far as to say that Kennedy was shot by someone who had sympathies with Cuba and who believed, it appears from his actions, that he had some kind of particular role to play, but we do not unfortunately know what it was. Interestingly enough all these people were shot in public, according to methods prevalent at the time—in fact in Kennedy's case the well-known film *The Manchurian Candidate*, which is about the shooting of a prominent political figure in a public place by very much the same method as Oswald employed, was actually then on general release in the United States. So, in other words, the point that we derive from cases of political assassination is that it is certainly possible to shoot prominent members of governments in this way, purely because of the assassin's minimal political contact; the fact that they are politically-motivated actions is interesting but the methodology is substantially different from that of, for example, the coup.

Now to take a textbook example of the coup proper— a barracks revolt in which there was no opposition—Finer offers us Batista's seizure of power in Cuba in 1952 (Finer 1962). To begin with, the action here started at precisely 2.43 a.m. This follows the old military dictum that you never start at 2.00, because that means, particularly in Latin America, that people would turn up at any time between 2.00 and 3.00, whereas if you start at 2.43 there is a fair chance the action will have begun at least by 2.45. At exactly 2.43 a.m. on 10 March 1952 Batista was already, as Commander-in-Chief of the forces, in position at the main military headquarters, Campo Colombia. From there he co-ordinated the simultaneous capture of the barracks at Campo Colombia itself and La Cabana with the aid of both the airforce and naval forces standing by, gunboats ready to shell and bombers ready to bomb. The whole action was over in one hour and seventeen minutes precisely. In that time the troops involved had seized all the main strategic points, occupied the airport to stop the government getting away, occupied the trade-union headquarters (rather grandiloquently known as the Workers' Palace) and, for some reason known only to themselves, Havana University. Thus all the main centres of political power in Cuba were covered. By 6.30 a.m. there was a small volume of firing at the presidential palace which killed two people. This was a hint to the president that it was time for him to go into exile by the approved route. At 8.30 a.m. he fled. In the course of the morning the new government was announced, and business began as usual on 11 March 1952.

It was therefore only a little over twenty-four hours before the country was back to normal and the new government formed. The military here were wholly loyal to Batista, supported him throughout and there was co-ordination with both the navy and airforce, the sort of thing, in other words, that was probably only possible for Commanders-in-Chief. And there was therefore no substantial opposition; what firing there was, was almost entirely symbolic.

But when there is opposition, where, in other words, there

are military forces established that intend to resist any seizure of power, a different situation arises, such as happened in Ghana in 1966. The leader here was a high military official, Colonel A. A. Afrifa, operating in collaboration with the police, who in turn knew that there was going to be strong opposition from the presidential guard. For the Ghanaian Presidential Guard had been deliberately trained in Eastern Europe, as opposed to the regular Ghanaian army which had been trained in Britain, and had therefore been set up as President Nkrumah's personal bodyguard independent of other forces with which they had no direct connection. (The same kind of situation, incidentally, existed in Indonesia at the time of the fall of Sukarno.) The establishment of a highly professional presidential guard, very heavily armed indeed, was of course a major tactical obstacle (Afrifa 1966). So how did the military set about it?

First of all, they were able to carry out their plans much more easily than would otherwise have been the case because they were supposed to prepare an expeditionary force to go to the Congo to establish the power of Nkrumah there. They were therefore able to carry out all their regular military manœuvres and plan the operation under the cover of preparing to go to the Congo. They had transport and everything available laid on. Secondly, they waited until Nkrumah had actually gone out of the country so that there would be that much less opposition and also to avoid the embarrassment of killing him, which would have been very awkward politically. And then they did not tell any of their followers what they were going to do. They sent them out on a tactical military exercise and told them half-way down the road that in fact what they were going to do was to capture the presidential residence, and they went ahead and did so as if at Sandhurst —they were all Sandhurst-trained officers! And again the whole operation went very quickly, except that on this occasion the capture of both Christiansborg Castle and Flagstaff House, which was Nkrumah's residence and therefore very heavily guarded, was attended by very heavy casualties on both sides. But elsewhere there was no other substantial opposition. One of the important points was that the military had waited until they had discovered that there was no real chance of civilian resistance. In the event it proved there was, on the contrary, quite considerable civilian support for their action. After that they only had to eradicate what military resistance there was and then they were in effective control.

Finer also describes the rapid seizure of power in Costa Rica in 1870 by Tomás Guardia. The key point that Finer makes about the episode is that he believes that Guardia was a civilian. He was not: he was a soldier and held the rank of colonel. What he did, was to arrange eleven other men concealed in two haycarts with two men beneath and ten others disguised as itinerant vagabonds, pedlars, etc., following behind—a total of twenty-four men. Pedro Quiros, a currier, presented himself one morning at the gate of the artillery barracks at which he worked and when admitted hit the sentry over the head, propped the gates open, and let the haycarts in, Trojan Horse style. The men leapt out, disarmed all the soldiers and seized control of the artillery barracks. They were aided by the fact that all the officers were asleep, and all the officers were asleep because they had stayed up all night the night before, having been told that there was going to be a coup. Eventually they had given up waiting for it and had gone to sleep. So that was an undoubted help. By 9.40 a.m., Guardia's men had seized control of the barracks. The commandant and two officers, who were woken by the noise of the other officers being disarmed, realised that something was going on, shouted out and were killed in the process, though not before the commandant had managed to send off a messenger to warn the President of what was going on. The messenger would have warned the President if it had not been for the unfortunate fact that the President had gone out to take a morning walk. And so he missed him. The President was therefore actually arrested in the street on his morning constitutional. Tomás Guardia went on to be a very fine president of Costa Rica, carried out many reforms and in particular introduced universal education in his country (Monge Alfaro 1966).

This incident is what Finer calls a Golpe, a very quick seizure of power in which the question of political support is not much considered—it is regarded as being neutral.

There are no prior bargains. Also, it is not a regular barracks revolt because it is not carried out by an officer of the hierarchy and is not a straightforward seizure of power by the military, or a displacement of government. This is a case of a person, who happens to be a soldier, making use of the military process in order to seize power.

To emphasise the role of prior preparation we shall consider also the action phase of three incidents that were very badly prepared. The first is the attempt by the communist party to seize power in 1965 in Indonesia (Hughes 1968). It took place, evidently, on the lines of a contingency plan that they had prepared for the event of Sukarno's death, and with the experience of two previous attempts to seize power, both disastrous failures. This case is unique and there has been up to now no such example in any other part of the world—it seems to have been a local aberration. Sukarno was known to be ill; he suffered from kidney trouble and was definitely regarded as being in a very poor state of health. For years he had balanced the military on one hand against the communists on the other and each against the religious party (the Ulama) on the third. He alone had the ability to balance these three, and it was well known that when he died this would have to be resolved.

In fact Sukarno collapsed suddenly in the middle of a speech in public. He did not die; in fact he recovered within a couple of hours; but in the meantime some of those present believed that he had died, that he had actually suffered a heart attack, and that this was the moment to strike. They warned Aidit, the Secretary General of the PKI, who ordered the initiation of the contingency plan. Communist forces seized six of the most senior generals of the Indonesian army, murdered them and threw their bodies down a well. They proceeded to seize a number of possible strong points. But there were two peculiar cases which suggest haste. First of all, they did not know where the generals were. The most senior, Nasution, was not in his house at the time. They murdered his wife and children, but did not succeed in capturing him, thus leaving him, the senior general in the Indonesian army, at large. (Tragically, he was so upset by the loss of his wife and children that he never recovered.)

And the second peculiar case was the case of Suharto, subsequently President of Indonesia. Suharto had been warned by a soothsayer, an astrologer, that he was to go on a particular night to a place where the waters met and say his prayers. So he did; he went out in a small boat to the mouth of the river and spent all night in prayer. When he came back he discovered the city in absolute uproar—many of the leading generals murdered, all kinds of upheaval. He took command of the army, mopped up, and in the course of the next few weeks there was an appalling massacre of everyone who was in any way suspected of communist sympathies. In other words, what happened was that the contingency plan had not allowed for the effective action of anyone who had escaped, particularly a senior military officer. The army strike failed and therefore the whole revolt collapsed, and it was the army who in the end, with their reserve of force, were able to survive. (Hughes 1968, see also Vittachi 1967.)

A second interesting example is the Bay of Pigs. No one at the time seems to have seen it for what it was: an attempt to seize political power. Considered in that light it is clear that almost every conceivable mistake was made. If its instigators wanted to seize political power they were especially foolish to announce to the Cubans that the expedition was on its way and that they ought to rise against Fidel Castro, who, as it happened, was quite popular at that stage. So the announcement merely served to destroy the advantage of surprise without bringing any other advantages (Johnson 1965).

A third case was that of the airforce revolt in Guatemala in 1962. Here the airforce tried to seize power by bombing the presidential palace. The President, an army general, carrying a machine gun under one arm, went out followed by supporters with a few heavy machine guns and tanks and mopped up the airfield defence. Then when the planes landed they merely put them out of action and arrested their crews (Ydígoras Fuentes 1963). And that was the end of the airforce revolt. A year later, in 1963, the same President was overthrown in a few hours in a bloodless coup, but this time the coup was planned and executed by the army.

At first sight there does not, perhaps, seem to be much in common between these events and the great social revolutions which are usually agreed to have been of major significance. But in practice the same analytical distinctions can be applied in those cases too. The difference is that they are formed, not of single events, but of a chain or sequence of events in which political power is transferred from one group to another. Naturally such sequences display a considerable degree of continuity, and this often leads historians of individual sequences to assume a degree of overall inevitability in the way events turn out.

It is precisely here that the comparative study of revolution comes into its own, for it enables us to compare such sequences, which did promote major socio-economic changes, with many other sequences which did not. Such sequences, typically, fail to result in the classic polarisation of opinion and the build-up of increasingly radical coalitions favouring change. Instead they display the characteristic pattern of alternating coups, frustrating the build-up of a consistent coalition and leading to a political stalemate.

A critic might say that it does not look as if there was a great deal of preparation for the Great Revolutions themselves. Is this question relevant to them too? Indeed, the point is that most of the time there was in fact very wide public support for what appeared at the time to be relatively minor adjustments. In other words, with the hindsight of history *we* can see Napoleon rising to power: first of all the artillery officer of 1795, then the Consul of 1799, then the Emperor of 1804. We can see this all happening, because we live now. But at the time it did not appear like this to the people who were actually watching it take place.

The second point is that there were also some very sharp reversals even in these revolutions. One of the interesting things about them is that although you can break them down into a series of coup-like events—short moments in which political power actually changed from one group to another— you see also at the same time evidence of the difference between pre-planning and luck. For example, the attempt to overthrow Robespierre was extremely badly pre-planned indeed. His opponents virtually seized him in a panic, for fear of their own lives. Their preparations were poor, and in fact, had Robespierre himself not been disabled by a luckily-placed shot in the jaw which made him incapable of speech, he would probably have retained political power, and could even have strengthened his position, as indeed he had done earlier in the same evening when, first arrested, he was rescued by his friends. It was only at the second attempt to seize him that the action succeeded, and with a modern secret police that attempt would have been forestalled.

When the Rump was dissolved in England in 1653 it was a neat military operation, Cromwell having placed plenty of soldiers all round the House of Commons. But in 1659 when the military attempted to do the same thing again and to enforce their will upon parliament, it simply did not work. The people would take no more army rule. What people had come to accept was the idea of the Restoration, so that when General Monck 'pronounced' in favour of the monarchy at Coldstream, he found an enormous body of public support. All he had to do was to march slowly to London, waiting for that support to strengthen, and the military leaders in London were quite outflanked.

In effect, you can apply the same principles to almost any situation. Once sequences have been broken down into their component revolutionary events, it is possible to see their common basis in the gathering of political support and its translation into military terms and into a successful revolutionary event. For such an event to be successful it must have leadership, recruit support, have access to material facilities (e.g. weapons, transport), and have well-defined goals capable of being translated into action. Of these, leadership and recruitment will be discussed in detail in Chapter 5, and the question of material facilities, and the part foreign governments and others play in the provision of them, will form an important theme of later chapters.

CONSOLIDATION

Once political power has been seized, its holders face the problem of its consolidation. This is, ironically, the part of the revolutionary process most lacking in a theoretical framework, and yet it is the key to the relationship between the fact of political revolution and the aspiration to social change.

Once again we shall find it helpful to begin with the consolidation of the coup. When a coup has taken place there are then two major objectives for the coup promoters. Firstly, there is what Goodspeed calls the 'pursuit stage', the eradication of serious opposition. This makes use of three principal devices: the establishment of martial law; the setting up of revolutionary tribunals to try the enemies of the state, and/or the establishment of a secret police organisation; or the use of an existing police organisation, to hunt down any potential political enemies.

Secondly, there comes the mobilisation of general support with or without the acquisition of legitimacy. The acquisition of legitimacy is highly desirable but it is not always easy, and many governments have found the best method is simply to constitute themselves as a provisional government and go on running the country. For as long as they are provisional there is always the hope that they may eventually go away.

Devices that are constantly used in all kinds of military coups for mobilising general support include some or all of the following. Firstly, price and wage fixing: there is no question of fixing prices without wages or wages without prices—the army fix both, and the usual remedy is to shoot anybody who gets out of line. Secondly, there is the stabilisation of the revolutionary forces themselves. If these were left unchanged, there would immediately be a problem with the existing regular military forces who are usually too strong to be wholly disarmed and too conservative to be taken over. If it is a military coup, in any case, they will not allow themselves to be taken over, so the forces that have been mobilised for the purpose of taking over power must be stabilised; that is, either demobilised or incorporated into regular units. And the transfer of law and order to disciplined bodies, properly established police or militia forces is of great importance because as long as there is a purely *ad hoc* martial law, too many people will be in a state of fear for the economic system to function properly.

Two further stages of legitimation follow: thirdly, internal legitimation by plebiscite or election or the calling of some kind of convention; then (not necessarily last and certainly not the least important) comes external recognition—recognition by foreign powers. Now from the micro situation in the revolutionary situation proper (the consolidation of a 'great revolution') one can expect to find stages of evolution corresponding to these stages—the first and second stage certainly, possibly all four. Talmon (Talmon 1961) speaks of three stages in the evolution of the French Revolution; one is the stage of 'popular enthusiasm', two is the stage of 'Jacobin improvisation', and the third is the period of Babouviste crystallisation'. These are nice phrases to be considered in turn.

'Popular enthusiasm' means spontaneous mass rising at the beginning—the storming of the Bastille. Then it is necessary to create a more stable form of government and this was done by setting up the Committee of Public Safety, the Reign of Terror and so forth, which Talmon calls 'Jacobin improvisation'. 'Babouviste crystallisation' reflects the crystallising of a set of ideas and social programmes in the aftermath of the Revolution. The Babouvistes, followers of the radical leader Gracchus Baboeuf, were the extreme left faction who were suppressed by the Jacobins and ultimately by the Directory. The development of popular participation in the French Revolution, as in the Russian Revolution, and in a number of the other great revolutions has been slow. The immediate aftermath of the revolution has been a period of provisional government marked by martial law, revolutionary tribunals and the establishment of a secret police, but not a phase of terror—yet. The immediate position is the setting up of a provisional government which is supposed to be more representative—more representative that is, than the government that went before. The turning towards terror, however, is precipitated by two things—firstly, a consciousness that the internal forces acting against the revolution are stronger than were at first thought, and that this is contrary to the predictions, the ideological predictions of the promoters of the revolution. And secondly, in all the great terrors— the French Revolutionary Terror, the Red/White Terrors in Russia—there is also a combination of internal opposition with external attack or foreign threat. In the case of the French Revolution it can be dated to the assassination of Marat; in the case of the Russian Revolution, the attempted assassination of Lenin. Up to that time, such Terrors as there had been in Russia were principally White rather than Red.

Brinton (Brinton 1952) regards terror as resulting from a combination of traditional violence; civilian militarism (that is, the desire of the civilians to subordinate themselves to a truly efficient government with military overtones); the inefficiency of the extremist government itself; an acute economic crisis complicated by class struggle; and religious hysteria.

So the first stage after the change of government is a limited degree of consolidation, the eradication of serious opposition, followed, in this particular case, by terror. And terror is followed, in turn, by Thermidor, a period of relaxation; decline of persecution, the collapse of moral sanctions, the restoration of government on the old basis and the end of plebiscitary democracy. Psychologically this would be the understandable consequence of the effects of being 'forced to be free'.

Some of these phenomena are extremely interesting; for example, the socially beneficial consequences of price and wage fixing which was one of the elements in the French Revolution. There were also adverse ones from the creation of a new currency by the issue of *assignats*, the difficulties of inflation, and so forth being met by government action for the first time in modern history. These were then followed by a number of much more widespread social changes in the French Revolutionary situation—the same happened again in Russia.

Most striking is the destruction and re-creation of the national community and of the family from which it is derived. The execution of the monarch, destruction of the aristocracy and elimination of the church as a force in politics combine to destroy the 'national family', the hierarchical structure of government. The sweeping away of religious and legal moral sanctions in both cases accompanies the process, atomising the family and giving the state a direct relationship to the individual. Here too there could be contradictions; in the early days of the Soviet Union the formal rise in the status of women was accompanied by permissive legislation on marriage, divorce and abortion but not by a lasting gain in full political equality. In fact, by 1934 the Stalin regime was enacting a new puritanism which in many respects echoed a similar reaction during the Napoleonic period in France. Such a reaction is of course not confined to revolutionary situations. In England, for example, the Victorian period embodied a clear middle-class reaction against the libertarian aristocratic manners of the Regency period, and Pitrim Sorokin, among sociologists, has sought to relate all the major political events of war and revolution to an underlying oscillation in history between the 'ideational' and the 'sensate' society (Sorokin 1937). But the significance of this must be seen in a deliberate attempt to return to the old ways, by stabilising the structure of the family to re-stabilise that of the political community as a whole, and, inevitably, to reintroduce the concept of hierarchy—in the Russian case most dramatically shown by the reintroduction of uniforms for state employees.

The sharper the reaction, however, the greater the likelihood of despotism. Brinton (1952) believes that Russian despotism owes more to Asia than to reaction, but Napoleon cannot be explained away in this fashion. The point is that in this case, as in others, it is clear that the pre-revolutionary state has most in common with the post-revolutionary state. The ultimate post-revolutionary state is remarkably like the pre-revolutionary state except that there is a considerable amount of social engineering in between. Secondly, the great revolutions are few in number, precisely because the exact combination of internal civil strife, with foreign intervention, without a precise military conclusion resulting, is exceedingly rare.

Normally one or other of three possibly scenarios may be expected to occur instead: that the military intervention is successful; that it is completely repulsed; or that the internal civil war is resolved, one way or the other. And in modern times what is noticeable is that most violent changes in power are taking less and less time, and as this time gets shorter and shorter, so the chances of external intervention get smaller and smaller. It may even be that the great powers have become wise to the fact that if there is one aspect of the revolutionary situation they can control, it is that they can always stay out of it. Looking at what politicians are capable of on subjects they are alleged to know something about, like economics, one can understand why they cannot be expected to know much about revolutions.

And the last point is that it does appear that the whole sequence is really tragically primitive. It is far from clear that it helped French society one whit, to slaughter its aristocrats. It does not seem that the massacres in Russia or in Indonesia have done anyone any good. What is really curious is that they should happen at all—this extraordinary facility that human beings have for killing large numbers of their own species. It has been suggested that in fact this relates directly to the nature of political power. Elias Canetti, in *Crowds and Power* (1973), says that the ultimate experience of political power is to have lots of people lying around dead in front of you, as described by Gabriel García Marquez in *One Hundred Years of Solitude* (1978). Whether it derives from some kind of perversion or misapplication of the hunting instinct or not he does not really consider. But he does point out that there is a very interesting symbolism associated with prostration before the ruler, for example: the elevation of the ruler in relation to those around him, but most emphatically in those primitive cultures where the fact of rulership is acknowledged by complete prostration, with the subject people lying down. He continues with the point that this kind of utter subjection of one's enemy feeds the appetite for power very drastically. Once the ruler actually sees the bodies lying around him he then goes megalomaniac very swiftly. The anthropological evidence that power is very directly related to large-scale massacres is too alarmingly like the Russian Revolution and the French Revolution for us to ignore it altogether.

2 Force in the international system

As noted above, the traditional view of international relations was that it was concerned primarily with the formal relations between the legal entities known as states. The state itself, as the legally constituted expression of the political community, had both the authority and, if it could command it, the power to ensure its will was obeyed within its own borders. What determined the relations between states, however, was a matter of some controversy. Legally each state was characterised by three attributes: sovereignty, territorial integrity and legal equality. In practice, governments intervened constantly in the affairs of their neighbours, the map of Europe was redrawn after each major war in accord with the demands of the victors, and weaker states might lose huge tracts of territory to stronger ones (Luxembourg) or even disappear altogether (Poland).

Before the emergence of the modern European state system it had been assumed that behind every system of state law lay divine law or 'natural law'. This view was most comprehensively rejected by Thomas Hobbes, whose pessimistic view of man in the state of nature was shared by many observers of the international state system, who saw the relations between states as being essentially ungoverned and ungovernable. The older view survived, to be restated in more modern terms by Immanuel Kant, who held that there were in fact universal moral imperatives governing human behaviour even in the absence of governmental sanction. His tract *Perpetual Peace* was the first important work on international relations written by a philosopher rather than by a diplomat or an international lawyer. It was not, however, acceptable to the practitioners of international relations, on the grounds that they could not make bargains with people when they had no assurance that they would be kept.

Consequently, what has come to be the dominant view of international relations in the modern world is what may be termed the Grotian view, after Hugo Grotius, perhaps the best-known of a number of writers on international law in the seventeenth century who established the view that international society was neither anarchy nor an idealised political community, but a structure of self-interested agreements which it was in the common interest of the contending parties to maintain. Under this view, the breach of any agreement threatened the credibility of the structure of the whole; it was therefore in the common interest to maintain the whole to ensure the effectiveness of any bargain, even if that was not seen as being immediately and directly in one's own interests at that particular moment, or even at all.

The international community is, in the words of Hedley Bull, an 'anarchical society' (1977)—a society or community which is at the same time different from national communities in the weakness of its formal rules and the difficulty of enforcing them. It may be worth noting, however, that in the past some national communities survived for long periods unaltered in such a condition, and indeed that the development of strong national governments certain of being able to enforce their wishes in the vast majority of cases, is a relatively recent historical development. Furthermore, since the beginning of the twentieth century an important qualitative change has come over the system, contemporaneously with the extension of the European system to the entire world. For the first time in human history an elaborate network of organisations has been slowly developed to avoid, rather than to resolve, international differences. Of these the most important, as well as the best-known, is the United Nations Organisation.

The United Nations is not a world government. It has no forces at its disposal to enforce its decisions, and such forces as have been raised for special purposes in localised areas (Cyprus, the Gaza strip) depend on their continued existence on the resolutions of the member stages and, even more importantly, on the willingness of the richer powers to pay for their maintenance. For the United Nations, unlike a national government, has no taxing power of its own. Worst of all, although its very existence is supposed to represent the rejection of force in the settlement of disputes between nations, its Charter does in fact specifically legitimate the use of force in 'self-defence' as well as in pursuance of a decision made collectively, and so legitimises a state in frustrating the purposes for which the organisation was set up. It is only fair to say that this provision of the Charter was part of the necessary process of political bargaining by which the organisation was set up, and it is undoubtedly much better to have the organisation with this weakness than not to have it at all.

The Charter, therefore, in some respects consolidates and in others modifies the structure of international relations as it had grown up in the three centuries since 1648. What it did not do was to supersede it entirely. States continued to be legally sovereign, as witness the provisions that the United Nations could not intervene in their internal affairs, and any violation of their territorial integrity continued to be regarded as a legitimate pretext for the use of force even if that violation was purely technical. Attempts of the smaller states, who increasingly came to dominate the proceedings of the General Assembly after 1960, to have their legal equality taken seriously, were not successful; and the more unequal they became, the more hostility came to be polarised between the wealthy and developed 'North' and the poor and underdeveloped 'South', adding new and dangerous grounds for conflict to those that had already developed between the East and West camps of the Cold War period in which the United Nations had taken shape.

The fundamental point about the use of force in the international system of today, therefore, is that it is almost universally regarded as legitimate. It is legitimate, moreover, not just for the world community as a whole but for each and every one of the national actors concerned. There is, in consequence, a considerable range of ways in which states and other actors use force within the international order in pursuit of their individual objectives. We note in particular:

(a) subversion;
(b) demonstrations of force;
(c) military aid;
(d) military intervention;
(e) war.

SUBVERSION

Since the time of Machiavelli, and indeed long before, states have sought to pursue their national goals within the international order by converting other states to their way of thinking. Such actions, where they are aimed at installing new governments, are often described (at least by the old governments) as subversion (cf. Greig 1973). But subversion, like beauty, is in the eye of the beholder. There is a very narrow line between diplomats who involve themselves closely with current events in order to report on them more accurately, and diplomats who seek to change those events; and the line is not always easy to ascertain in practice.

Since it is an assumption of the international system that the state has the right to be free of interference in its internal affairs, the fact is that anything that can be construed as interference may be resented and give grounds for the use of force in return. Most, if not all, states use their police power to check actions that they regard as falling in this category. Some maintain large counter-intelligence organisations and even develop secret police forces, who differ from intelligence organisations in seeking to promote not just a negative acceptance of the regime, but a positive enthusiasm for it.

Even in such states popular participation in government is seen as legitimate, and indeed as an essential part of the government's claim to political authority. The same is true for almost all the current members of the United Nations, whether or not it is in fact effective. Consequently, states find it useful to engage in propaganda directed at the notional ultimate authority in target states; to appeal, to put it more briefly, over the heads of the government to the people. Obviously this can in itself be seen as an act of subversion. So too, in fact, can any statement on behalf of a foreign government, where, as so frequently happens, an act of revolution forms part of the essential legitimising myth by which that country identifies itself as an actor in world politics. There are, in short, no hard and fast lines between legitimate intercourse between nations and subversion. This is not, of course, to say that a direct incitement to revolt against an incumbent government, however evil that government may be, must be accepted by that government as legitimate. Such behaviour clearly lies outside the acceptable limits of the international system as legally constituted, however morally just it may appear to be to its proponents.

As will be discussed further in Chapter 7, clandestine activities designed to promote a country's cause, though technically improper, are also extensively used by the major and some minor powers. Some, such as the payment of bribes or 'subsidies' to individual politicians or political parties, have such a long ancestry that they may be regarded almost as hallowed by custom; at least as far as international practice is concerned, for they may—as in the United States —be prohibited by domestic legislation. Others, such as the gathering of information about another country's military capabilities, though illegitimate and severely punishable in time of war, are in peacetime regarded as almost routine, and punished in the case of diplomats only by expulsion or the token withdrawal of diplomatic representation. From this, some theorists have argued that such exchange of information is actually of positive value to the maintenance of the international order, since it helps ensure that countries are accurately informed as to one another's force capabilities. Support for 'peace' movements has in recent years been a marked feature of Soviet policy, aimed once again at using the formal structure of political representation to secure policies more favourable to Soviet military interests, and to strengthen its international bargaining position. None of these actions, though often regarded as subversive by the target states, is in fact likely in any way to bring about a change of government there. Such actions are very specific, and are likely to form part of a much wider strategy for the use of force.

DEMONSTRATIONS OF FORCE

The first requirement for the use of force in international relations is that states maintain armed forces on a permanent basis. Almost all modern states do this, one of the few exceptions being the Central American state of Costa Rica, where the armed forces were disbanded after the Revolution of 1948 in order to end the threat of militarism. Even the most improbable countries maintain armed forces, such as, for example, the Pyreneean state of Andorra, with an army of six men which fulfils, it must be said, a purely symbolic function.

Symbolism must not be discounted, however, since it is precisely in the symbolic evidence of the ability to defend themselves against foreign attack that most states see their best protection. In the past, the symbolic demonstration was enough, in that military threats could only be made effective through mobilisation, and that in itself gave sufficient time to mobilise in return. Conversely, the deployment of forces by a larger power, or the actual implementation of a mobilisation plan, might be sufficient in itself to bring about a desired change of policy in a neighbouring state. Thus in 1907 President Theodore Roosevelt sent the American fleet on a world cruise to avert the escalation of conflict with Japan. But in 1914 Austria mobilised with the ostensible purpose of bringing about a change of policy in Serbia, though actually with the intention of invading it and ending the threat it presented to the multinational Habsburg State by actual subjugation.

There are numerous examples of cases where the mobilisation or deployment of forces by great powers have in themselves been sufficient to affect the course of revolutionary events. In 1903 United States warships were deployed to make clear to Colombia that the United States was prepared to defend the independence of secessionist Panama. In 1910 United States warships were again deployed to favourably influence a change of government in Nicaragua, an event well remembered in that country when in 1983 the United States government under President Reagan carried out large-scale manœuvres in Honduras at a time when it was already supporting attacks by counter-revolutionary forces based in Honduras against the Sandinista government of Nicaragua.

Technically, mobilisation of forces or the conduct of military manœuvres in no way infringes international law, unless the state concerned is party to a treaty or agreement specifically forbidding such actions in the area where they are being conducted. Such treaties demilitarising specific zones for specific purposes have a long history, and were of particular importance in the regulation of international waterways such as the Dardanelles, the Black Sea and the Baltic Sea, and in establishing the international consensus on the neutrality of Switzerland, Belgium, Finland and Austria (1955). The acute state of permanent readiness of the modern superpowers, however, makes the question of indirect threats of this kind a much more difficult one to assess, and the problem is compounded by the extensive evidence of clandestine involvement by both the superpowers in domestic conflict in a number of countries.

Hence today 'demonstrations of force' can be achieved in the most indirect fashion by cryptic references to this state of permanent readiness incorporated in politicians' speeches or media pronouncements in close juxtaposition to references to the situation to be influenced. It is scarcely surprising, therefore, that an extensive mythology has grown up on both sides about the actual involvement of the rival superpower in a wide range of political events where such involvement has not subsequently been proved. Examples of this are the United States' charges of Soviet involvement in events in the Dominican Republic in 1965, and Soviet charges of United States involvement in events in Afghanistan in 1979.

MILITARY AID

Military aid to allies and client states is exceedingly ancient, and was incorporated naturally in the structure of the modern world system through its extensive practice in Europe before 1815 and in the construction of the European world empires. Thus, military aid to the princely states formed an important part of the strategy of the construction of the British Indian Empire, and in French penetration of Indo-China.

Aid, whether in the form of arms or their cash equivalent, is a perfectly legitimate transaction in international law where it involves support for an established government recognised by the international community. In such circumstances it can be, and is, carried on perfectly openly, and in no way constitutes an interference by the donor state in the internal affairs of the country concerned. This is not to say, however, that it may not have consequences for the recipient state that an impartial observer might not regard as extremely unfortunate, if not disastrous. The United States military aid to the last Shah of Iran, Reza Pahlevi (1941–79) strengthened his increasingly dictatorial rule against his political opponents and fostered an uncontrolled desire for even greater military expenditure that had disastrous effects on the Iranian economy. It played a major role in consolidating the opposition coalition that brought about the fall of the Shah in the Iranian Revolution of 1979. Thus, it was counterproductive in that the Revolution itself resulted in a partial 'reversal of alliances' on the part of the new regime.

Similarly, Soviet military aid to the Cuban Revolutionary Government has involved it ultimately in a long-term open-ended commitment which has proved exceedingly expensive. The deployment of Cuban forces in 1975 in Angola and Ethiopia, though perhaps beneficial to the Soviet Union in strategic terms, and certainly valuable in the sense of testing weapons in real combat conditions, has contributed to the militarisation of the Cuban government and the distortion of the Cuban economy which a prolonged military commitment involves. Soviet military aid to the governments of Eastern Europe, and the structure of alliance based on it, resulted in the fear of revolution that led to Soviet intervention in Czechoslovakia in 1968 and the enunciation of the Brezhnev Doctrine, by which the Soviet Union is committed to the maintenance of socialist governments and the irreversibility of Soviet-inspired revolutionary change.

MILITARY INTERVENTION

Military intervention can, therefore, be of two kinds; either by 'invitation' in support of an incumbent regime, which is generally acceptable under international law, or to give support in the most definite and uncompromising fashion possible to an opposition movement, which, though sanctioned in certain instances (e.g. Palestine) by resolutions of the United Nations, cannot yet be said to be generally acceptable under international law.

The relationship between military aid and intervention, on

the one hand, and between military intervention and other sorts of intervention, on the other, is a complex one. This topic is therefore dealt with in more detail in Chapter 8.

Military intervention in revolutionary incidents or events has historically often been the trigger for a general war, and such wars have been particularly characteristic of the periods of the so-called 'great social revolutions' (Pettee 1938). Thus, the English Civil War was followed by wars between England and foreign-backed forces in Ireland, as well as Scotland and the Dutch Republic. The French Revolutionary Wars (1793–1803) resulted from the intervention of the other European powers (the Netherlands, Britain, Austria, Prussia and Spain) in support of the monarchists. The Allied intervention in Russia in support of the White forces contributed powerfully to the radicalisation of the Revolution, and stimulated, rather than allayed, the desire of its leaders to win friends by propagating revolution in Europe and the Far East.

WAR

In fact each of these movements owed its origins, at least in part, to the defeat in war of the pre-revolutionary government. For war is a distinguishing characteristic, if not the distinguishing characteristic, of the international system, and the international system is structured by past generations' successive attempts to limit war without, however, relinquishing the right to resort to it in their own self-defence!

War as a contest carried on by force of arms necessarily implies the death of one's opponents. This presents two sorts of problems. Moral problems are raised by the idea of killing individuals who have in themselves done nothing to 'deserve' it. Wars, therefore, are justified by their participants in terms of self-defence, self-protection or the subhuman (i.e. inhuman) nature of their opponents. Practical problems arise from the obvious dangers of uncontrolled war. War has, therefore, to be legitimised by some authority acting on behalf of divine providence or the political community, or both.

The idea of war is therefore inextricably linked with the concept of the state. This is, however, not, as is often thought, because war is (or has been) an activity solely carried on by states. Rather, the state is the term that we give to the political community when it is organised for war. To conduct war, therefore, is to claim the role of a state, the sole entity that can legitimise an activity that in almost all societies of any complexity would be regarded as illegitimate if practised by an individual or group on its own account. Armed attempts to overthrow state governments may, therefore, be regarded as a form of 'internal war' (Eckstein 1964). The popular term 'civil war', also, has the connotation of being at one and the same time a major upheaval and one which has the political objective of seizing control of the state as constituted, and would, therefore, like internal war, include unsuccessful movements if sufficiently large, but exclude many events in which only small force levels were involved, but which can, as we shall see, lead to profoundly revolutionary consequences. Meanwhile, as far as the international system is concerned, states 'retain the monopoly of territory and the near-monopoly of large-scale legitimate force' (Frankel 1979, p. 55).

War presupposes the existence of weapons. However, until very modern times, weapons were not a specialised form of product designed purely for use in war, and only after the invention of gunpowder did they begin, and even then very slowly, to become so. This change accompanied the development of regular permanent military forces on a large scale. With the development came, for the first time, the need for large-scale plants designed for the exclusive purpose of producing munitions; and it was this, ironically, that was to lead strategists once more to break down the distinction between military and civilian in their urgency to stop-up the sources of military power by strategic bombing. The development of atomic weapons has altered this position in only one respect: that the states on both sides have grown to such an extent that sane military planning assumes the operation of deterrence rather than of retaliation, despite the moral problem that for deterrence to be effective, the other side has first to be convinced that its opponent will if necessary engage in retaliation that inevitably implies an appalling breach of widely-accepted principles of morality.

In one sense, therefore, nothing has changed. It is true, as has been remarked, that man now has the capacity to exterminate all human life with atomic weapons, but it has always been true that there have always been enough hands to strangle the entire human race. This had not deterred conflict, and it has not stopped wars. Only twice in the entire history of ancient Rome was the city of Rome at peace so that the temple gates of the god of war, Mars, could be closed. And in modern times Quincy Wright, in his major study, lists and analyses 278 wars that occurred in the period 1480–1941, wars of sufficient severity to result in substantial casualties (Wright 1965, p. 650: cf. Richardson 1960).

In other senses, however, nuclear capability does have important effects which are of special relevance to this discussion. Firstly, it creates the need, not just for weapons as such, but for complex weapons systems to ensure its maintenance, targeting and delivery. This in turn presupposes a close and constant relationship between government, the strategic armed forces and the manufacturers, the degree of whose specialisation is such that they are now wholly dependent on the one exclusive market for their product. Secondly, such systems are extremely expensive by any standards. In theory, a minimal nuclear capacity can be acquired relatively cheaply which will enable a state to impress its lesser neighbours; in practice it costs a great deal of money and makes that state an automatic target for one or other, and possibly both, of the superpowers. Meanwhile, the ability to maintain 'conventional forces' is correspondingly reduced for any given level of expenditure that may be contemplated. Thirdly, such highly specialised forces, and even more such ferociously powerful weapons, are of little or no use in the traditional alternative role of armed forces, namely counter-insurgency. A government cannot put down a rebellion with thermonuclear weapons, and indeed the use of tanks, artillery shells and conventional bombers may prove counter-productive, as witness the events leading up to the fall of Anastasio Somoza Debayle in Nicaragua in 1978–9. Lastly, as the Falklands Crisis of 1982 demonstrated, nuclear weapons do not deter conventional aggression; so that President Reagan's naval manœuvres off Nicaragua in 1983, impressive as the hardware deployed may be in the abstract, lose much of their

credibility as a response to the alleged threat of subversion or
guerrilla attack.

It can be argued, therefore, that the possession of nuclear
weapons actually limits a power's ability to respond to
threats of insurgency, and support for this view may be
found not only in the history of the American war in Vietnam (the Second Indo-China War, 1965–1975) but also in the
way in which Britain, who had successfully contained
guerrilla threats in Malaya, Kenya and Cyprus, was forced to
contract her forces in the late 1950s and failed dismally to
respond to insurgency in Aden (now the People's Republic
of South Yemen) soon afterwards (Bell 1976).

Lastly, the possession of nuclear weapons does not, it
seems, end the long human tradition of glorifying combat
with other human beings and regarding it as the highest
expression of human courage and endeavour in the face of
overwhelming odds. Undoubtedly, the glorification of war
has on many occasions been adapted to the services of
revolutionary movements which, by terming their members
'soldiers' and their forces 'armies', seek to legitimise—
apparently at least in the eyes of their own supporters—
their political ends. Were it not for the glorification of force
in war, indeed, the glorification of force as a means for
settling other political disputes or realising other political
aspirations would be hardly conceivable.

The mystique of war contributes to revolution in other
ways too. Firstly, it places undue emphasis on the value of
obedience and the military way of operation in the course of
the general service of the state. It would be pointless to deny
that in many ways military training is of great value in other
occupations. But there are many in which it is not, and often
the authoritarian attitudes characteristic of traditional
military training prove a major obstacle to the survival of
military governments themselves. Politics involves the management of a subtle structure of reward and punishment,
persuasion and bargaining as well as command. Thus, the
imposition of military ideas can and does contribute to the
desire for revolutionary change in many instances.

It is a popular belief, secondly, among some conserva-
tives, that universal military training will create a massively

disciplined population capable of meeting the challenges of rapid economic growth and expansion. The evidence suggests the exact reverse; in fact such training undercuts the desire to do more than just get by; it emphasises the value of personal survival rather than the desire to take risks, which is essential to economic growth, by stimulating hitherto untried ideas. It creates a large number of individuals with a degree of resentment against a system that has taken up a crucial period of their young lives with at best inconsequential and at worst thoroughly unpleasant activity. Worst of all, some of these individuals will have gained, free of charge, something that they might otherwise have had to go far to find, sophisticated instruction in the use of modern weapons and an awareness of their tactical possibilities. Armies in particular, therefore, are a traditional training ground, not only for the practitioners of the military coup, but for those who take to the hills and become guerrillas, and for those who lead others to the barricades in urban insurrection.

MILITARISM

The belief that military values are the highest expression of human activity is a very ancient one, and it is not surprising therefore to find that it is very deep-rooted. Particularly interesting from the point of view of the student of revolution is the complex relationship between militarism among the military themselves and militarism among civilians.

Militarism is, in the words of Alfred Vagts,

'a domination of the military man over the civilian, an undue preponderance of military demands, an emphasis on military considerations, spirit, ideals and scales of value, in the life of states.' [Vagts 1959, p. 14]

Discipline, a strong sense of group mission and *esprit de corps* are indeed defining characteristics of well-trained military forces. Such a sense of pride could be expected to feed on success and to evaporate in face of failure. In fact, the reverse appears to be the case. The undue development of militarism among the armed forces characteristically occurs as a result of military setback or defeat. By the common psychological mechanisms of displacement and projection, responsibility for such defeats as, for example, the Egyptian defeat in the Arab–Israeli War of 1948–9, is transferred to the civilian government. It becomes, in fact, an argument for greater dedication to military values, not less.

Ultimately, this can become the motivation for direct military intervention in politics. It is important to note, therefore, that when Finer writes of military intervention in terms of the 'opportunity' and 'disposition' the military have to intervene, that in the strict sense the military (assuming they exist at all) always have the opportunity to intervene. Indeed, the fact of their existence means that they are always intervening, if only at Finer's lowest level of intervention, namely as a lobby. What is different about the armed forces as a lobby is the compelling nature of their arguments (that without increased defence expenditure the country would be laid open to its enemies) and the opportunity that they have, as a branch of government and perhaps the major spending branch at that, to push their case from within. As Finer correctly recognises, what is remarkable about the armed forces is not that they intervene, but that there are any countries in the world that are not subject to military governments! (Finer 1962, p. 4). 'The military possess vastly superior organisation', he argues. 'And they possess *arms*.'

The weakness of the military position is, however, concealed by the word 'superior'. Superior in what respect? Certainly superior to any other agency within the state in the ability to project force. But for how long and with what assurance? An army is an integral part of the state, and it depends for its continued viability and effectiveness on the support it receives for the role it assumes from the civilian population on which it depends. Only where this dependence is minimised, either by acquiescence, or by external support and/or funding, or by extreme weakness in terms of social cohesion of politically-expressive structures such as political parties, churches and secret societies, can the military forces be free to pursue their own ambitions. In practice, the desire for military government is as much a civilian phenomenon as a military one, and generals who seize power do so in alliance with and at the urging of prominent civilians representing powerful interests within the state.

We turn, therefore, to civilian militarism, defined by Vagts as: 'the unquestioning embrace of military values, ethos, principles, attitudes; as ranking military institutions and considerations above all others in the state' (Vagts 1959, p. 453) by civilians, even at the cost of their own lives and well-being. It is found, as he himself suggests, in its most pure and least contested form in the later stages of an international war, when the frenzy of patriotic fervour has reached the height at which no sacrifice seems unreasonable in pursuit of the ideal of victory, and it goes far to explain the, at best, weak differences observed by Wright and Haas between democracies and autocracies in their propensity to go to war (Wright 1965, pp. 828–41; Haas 1965).

Civilian militarism may involve acceptance of the military claim to pre-eminence. But it seems as if it may also develop independently, forcing the military, often in circumstances unsuitable for successfully waging war, to live up to the expectations suddenly thrust upon them. So we find civilian militarism not only in Germany but also in Britain in the First World War, and not only in Japan but also in the United States, in the Second. In both cases, the exigencies of war forced the substantial expansion of the horizons of government power, making natural after the war what had been regarded as dangerous hitherto. It is easy to think of such an expansion in purely administrative terms, and that is precisely how in general it has tended to be regarded. Much more important is the way in which a sustained high level of crisis consolidates support for an incumbent government, enabling it to sustain a continued war effort far beyond what might objectively be planned for in time of peace. But administrative considerations cannot altogether be overlooked. A key reason for the acceptance of military government is the desire to short-cut the complex and unpredictable bargaining procedures of a fragmented society, in which bureaucratic structures are only partly developed and administrative jobs are seen as the personal property of the individual office-holder. In such societies, and they are the majority of the world's societies, the military forces offer the one arbiter of politics to which powerful interests can appeal in order to liberate themselves from the bonds they feel are limiting their potential.

Military intervention, once secured, creates new problems. At the lowest level, reliance on unconstitutional use of force permits it to be used freely against individuals according to the whim of immediate military commanders.

At the medium level, recent experience shows that military concepts of national security, particularly when linked to interservice rivalry in the control of the political process, can lead to the unrestrained use of arrest, torture and execution against the supposed enemies of the regime.

But at this level and at the top level there is, once the armed forces are enthroned, no further arbiter to which appeal may be made, with the sole, intangible and all-too ineffective exception of international public opinion. In the age of superpower competition the operation of such international sanctions as exist against such regimes depends on the stand of the bloc leaders, the superpowers.

EFFECT OF THE SUPERPOWER BALANCE

Since the end of the Second World War and the inception of the Cold War, the superpowers have each in imitation of the other built up a bloc of allies and client states on which they count for support in the international organisations and alliance in the event of an actual confrontation. This latter role must now be regarded as obsolescent in view of the very reasonable doubt that exists as to whether a conventional non-nuclear war could be possible between the blocks. It is in any case believed to be the established Soviet belief that any such conflict must necessarily be waged as all-out war involving the actual use of nuclear weapons, and because of the great Soviet preponderance in conventional forces in the European theatre, NATO has consistently refused to rule out the option of a first use of nuclear weapons in response to an actual Soviet conventional attack.

At the outset of the Cold War the Soviet Union held to the traditional Marxist position that it was its duty to further the world socialist revolution without which the safety of the

Soviet Union itself could not in the end be guaranteed. All states that were not in alliance with the Soviet Union were held at this stage to be hostile. It was only after the Bandung Conference of 1955 that the Soviet Union gradually began to recognise the non-aligned countries, such as India and Indonesia, as not forming part of the Western bloc, though it remained policy to further their onward transition from the state of national revolution towards the socialist ideal. Between 1959 and 1961 Cuba moved into the Soviet orbit of its own volition, influenced by the heavy-handed diplomacy of the Eisenhower administration into seeking a rival protector. This confirmed the Soviet view that non-alignment could only be a temporary halfway stage towards socialism, and it has been the message of the Cuban government up to and during its period of leadership of the non-aligned movement to align its members with the Soviet Union—something that they have in fact resolutely resisted.

The logic of bloc formation since that time has meant that a number of limited conflicts in what has since become known as the Third World have, through superpower support for each of the two sides, developed into 'wars by proxy'— as in Vietnam, the Horn of Africa and Angola. Closely linked with these developments have been sudden changes of government, designed either to realign states (such as Cambodia in 1970) or to forestall such realignments (as in Guatemala in 1954 or, allegedly, in Afghanistan in 1979).

As a result, the hierarchy of superpower relations now stretches right down below the level of the nation state into the internal political processes of each and every country on the surface of the globe. Hence, in theory, any development anywhere can in principle lead to superpower confrontation. In practice, fortunately, these possibilities are limited by the scarcity of resources, the strategic values of the superpowers, the salience of issues at any one time, and the exigencies of domestic politics, more particularly in the case of the United States. Fortunately, too, the most important political development in the post-war system, namely the emergence of new states, is now formally almost at an end, and a new possibility of stability for the system as a whole must result from the ending of the age of wars of national liberation.

3 Wars of national liberation

Wars of national liberation are as old as recorded human history. The union of the three forest cantons of Switzerland (1291) and the rise of the Dutch Republic after 1581 each contributed to our modern notions of liberty and laid the foundation of thought for later attempts by communities to establish their own form of self-government. It is with the French Revolution in particular, however, that historians tend to associate the rise of that phenomenon known as nationalism which has so much affected the history of the last 150 years.

Nationalism is the belief that a nation, that is to say a community of persons united by a common religion, language and/or culture, should be expressed in political terms by the creation by its members of a state, a political entity independent of other political entities. It is because the statesmen and politicians of revolutionary France laid much emphasis in their public speeches on the concept of the French nation, as a ground for their legitimate exercise of political power, that this period is seen particularly to have influenced the identification of nationhood with statehood. Ironically, in French a very clear distinction is made to this day between the two concepts, whereas English, for example, confuses the two, and English-speakers talk of 'nationalisation' because they lack any comparable verb derived from the word 'state'. The French Revolution, too, is an important historical turning point for another reason. Before that time in Europe dynastic states created a sense of nation among their inhabitants. After that time, people who regarded themselves as nations, for example the Poles, the Germans and the Italians, sought to create new states for themselves (Minogue 1969, Seton-Watson 1977).

After 1945 a large number of new states came into existence as the nineteenth-century colonial empires fell apart and former colonies became independent. In 1983, of all the nineteenth-century empires, only that of Russia remains intact. Of those of Great Britain, France, the Netherlands, Belgium, Spain and Portugal only tiny fragments, mostly islands, remain, and the dissolution of the Portuguese colonial empire in the mid-1970s effectively marks the end of the main phase of decolonisation. The United Nations Committee on Decolonisation, the so-called Committee of 24, continues to occupy itself with the problem of a few remaining disputed territories, but its interest reflects the pressure of a few interested parties rather than any very important strategic anomaly. Such pressures not surprisingly meet with the near-automatic approval of the bulk of the members of the General Assembly, themselves ex-colonies.

Such disputes have been fertile ground for the two superpowers, as they manœuvre for political advantage and alliance in what has now become generally known as the Third World. Here history is interestingly at variance with public image. The United States was once 'the first new nation', and her war of national liberation, termed in the United States itself 'the American Revolution', both preceded the French Revolution and contributed to it, and has much in common with it. With its rise to world standing in the twentieth century, however, the United States has in much of the Third World come to be seen as a conservative power, maintaining a system of alliances with reactionary rulers in what many left-wing writers regard as a 'neo-imperialist' relationship. By this they mean that in place of the formal structures of nineteenth-century empire, from which the United States dissociated itself in the 1930s by promising independence to the Philippines, its only large overseas possession, there have grown up ties of financial investment and control which enable the United States to obtain the support she wants and to draw all the financial benefits she attributes to the possession of colonies.

The Soviet Union, on the other hand, is the successor state to the Russian Empire, acquired by military conquest and subjugation. It was created in 1922 as the political expression of the reconquest of those parts of Central Asia and Central Europe that tried to secede after 1917, and was added to by the military conquest of the Baltic States during the Second World War, and the annexation of large parts of

Poland and other frontier territories. The Soviet Union professes, however, to be a Marxist state, ideologically committed to the support of movements for national liberation, and ready at all times to denounce the United States as an 'imperialist' power, regardless of the latter's strong support for the dissolution of the European colonial empires. This view is often uncritically accepted in the Third World, where there is no history of recent Russian penetration and where some national liberation movements have, since 1945, been able to receive Soviet ideological, if not military, support. Since the United States has been officially precluded in many cases from following suit, owing to its alliance with the metropolitan powers concerned, the Soviet Union has been able to use this as support for its view of the United States as itself an 'imperialist' power.

The contest between the superpowers for influence among rival Third World states, and the problem of whether or not to support their aspirations, is not new. Very similar considerations underlay the concept of the 'balance of power' in Europe in the nineteenth century, and the pressure to create the European colonial empires in the first place. The position today is, however, complicated by the fact that, although in some places nationalism is a strong and potent force in the Third World, in other places, notably in Africa where the present state boundaries are the artificial creations of European statesmen and map-makers and so cut across religious, linguistic and ethnic boundaries, the existence of the state has again preceded the emergence of the concept of nation. To create such a concept has therefore been the work not only of charismatic nationalists such as Nkrumah in Ghana or Kenyatta in Kenya, but also of military administrators such as the successive leaders of Nigeria or of Somalia. All nationalism, to be successful, draws heavily on local symbolism, a sense of differentness. Hence its successful achievement creates a sense of individuality among such leaders and renders them much less willing than they might otherwise have been to enter any wider political grouping.

Such fragmentation has contributed to the division both of the African continent and of the Arab world. The latter is particularly remarkable, since the unifying effect of Islam has historically been strong, yet even with its heightened sense since the mid-1970s revival, the only issue that effectively still unites the Islamic states remains their hostility to Israel. With the effective ending of the period of the creation of new states, all such regional groupings are in any case now settling down into a more routine era of diplomacy, in which relationships are at least less likely to be disrupted by the emergence of any new counter in the power balance. The only remaining possibility for a sudden change of pattern, therefore, is a major revolution in one or other of the component states.

The age of wars of national liberation, however, will continue to influence such future developments, and it will therefore be useful to have a look at the special features of such wars. Wars of national liberation are a type of revolution in that they involve the seizure of power by the use of force. They differ from a purely internal event in that the goal sought is secession, the creation from a province of the former 'empire', of a new state as an independent actor in the international system. There are in fact several other ways in which states can become independent. States can become independent by attenuation, that is to say, the weakening of ties with the metropolitan state to the point at which the metropolitan authorities recognise that independence is already an accomplished fact: such states are, for example, Canada, Australia, and New Zealand. They can become independent by political negotiation and peaceful agreement —such as Norway, Iceland and the majority of British and French colonial territories since 1945—among them Ghana, Nigeria, Cameroon, Upper Volta and the Ivory Coast. In terms of recent history, this is now by far the commonest method by which independence has been achieved. They can, exceptionally, declare independence when separated from their mother country by the exigencies of war or the occupation of the metropolitan countries themselves. This was a major cause of the early movements towards independence in the Latin American states and was the determining factor in the independence of Syria and Lebanon in 1941. Only in a relatively small number of cases, thirty-six of the cases that occurred between 1901 and 1960 (Calvert 1970b, p. 139), was independence gained by the use of force or convincing threat of force by separatist movements, and these cases include those in which the force was provided by a state of international war.

Separatist movements have one great advantage over other revolutionists. Their goal of separatism is compatible with the survival of the incumbent government of the metropolitan country, which therefore need not press the fight to a conclusion and can if it wishes enter into negotiations for the termination of the active phase of conflict on terms acceptable to both sides. Such has been the pattern in the majority of cases since 1945, though in the case of Aden (South Yemen) and some of the ex-Portuguese territories no such settlement was in fact achieved before the metropolitan state decided to cut its losses by withdrawal.

As these cases remind us, separatist movements may, in addition, have the great advantage of operating in a territory that is not contiguous to the metropolitan state, and which the metropolitan government therefore finds it much harder to reinforce. Where, as in the case of Spain and Britain, the acquisition of sea power was an important factor in the creation of an empire, loss of sea power was an important factor in its dissolution. The British Empire was unusually dispersed. Most other imperial powers have sought to expand in a limited area of the world, either on land, like Russia or Austro-Hungary, or across inland sea as in the case of France or Italy, for each of which states such expansion represented the logical next stage of an expansion already completed on land. The loss of sea power was an important factor above all in the case of the Netherlands and Indonesia, where Britain had in fact helped reconquer Java at the conclusion of the Second World War, at one stage making use of the only troops available, namely the defeated Japanese! (Drummond 1979).

Where such separatist movements occur close to the territory of another major power or superpower the chances are great that they will receive clandestine support from that power, as in the case of China's support for the communists in Indo-China, between 1949 and 1954.

The disadvantages of separatist movements stem mainly

from their weakness in face of the strength of the metropolitan country. A country controlling a large empire is in
a position rather like a central bank: faced with pressure
from one direction at a time, it is in a position to bring to
bear such force that local interests cannot hope to compete
with it. Faced with pressure from all sides at once, it may have
no option but to give way. Thus, as J. Bowyer Bell (1976)
points out, Britain was in a relatively favourable position
after 1945 in that the challenges to its central power came
one after the other. Though the force at its disposal was not
always sufficient to overcome armed insurgency, therefore, in
almost all cases it was able to ensure a settlement more
favourable to its interests than would otherwise have been
the case. Bell identifies the cases of Ireland, Israel and India
as the three experiences that taught British governments to
develop flexible responses to the problem of disengagement,
showing them the advisability of creating representative
institutions with which negotiations for independence could
be successfully concluded and of avoiding the situation in
which the home government was directly confronting a direct
challenge to its own authority, such as was the case in
Palestine.

A consequential weakness of a successful separatist
movement may well be the fact that it stimulates in turn
provincial or regional demands for separatism, such as led
to the secession of Bangladesh from Pakistan and the unsuccessful moves for the secession of Biafra from Nigeria
or the Cabinda enclave from Angola. The history of Latin
America in the nineteenth century offers a particularly
striking series of examples of such a progression; from,
for example, the secession of New Granada from Spain,
to its dissolution into the three separate states of Colombia,
Ecuador and Venezuela, and finally to the secession of
Panama from Colombia, which was at the same time
constantly troubled by similar secessionist movements in
other provinces. In this respect the case of North-East Ulster/
Northern Ireland is not exceptional. What is unusual about
it is that its claim to separateness takes the form of
close identification with the metropolitan state, Great
Britain.

NATIONAL LIBERATION AND
THE INTERNATIONAL SYSTEM

To understand the relationship between national liberation and the international system it will first be necessary to consider further the historical development of the international system after the French Revolution.

Between 1815 and 1914 the world order was dominated by the great European Powers. Those in the centre of the Eurasian land mass expanded on land; those on its fringes by sea. They did so at the expense of non-European empires such as Turkey, Iran/Persia and China, as well as by the conquest and subjugation of 'unoccupied' territory. The term 'empire' itself has an interesting history. Originally, before 1805, there was only one European empire, the Empire, which had historically enshrined the universal concept of a world empire. By claiming the title of Emperor, Napoleon was therefore asserting a universal primacy; ironically it was this act which made the concept of empire a divisible one. Hitherto, the rulers of Turkey and Iran had been accorded their own special titles, as were the multitudinous rulers of the Indian states. Now to the rulers of China and Japan were added the formal titles of the rulers of France, Germany and Great Britain (in her person as Empress of India), and the new word 'imperialism' was coined to designate the desirability of creating and maintaining empires—only later was it to be reversed by Hobson (1902) and Lenin (1916) to give it an undesirable connotation (see Hobson 1968, Lenin 1967).

At the beginning of this long period new states came into existence that were accepted as such and did not become part of the great European empires. But the majority of them were concentrated in the Americas, where the isolation of distance and sea communication allowed a largely independent order to be established, without, however, challenging the existing possessions of European powers other than Spain and Portugal. Serbia (independent 1805) and Greece (independent 1822) maintained their independence in the disputed area between Turkey and Europe known as the Balkans, where they were to be joined in due course by

Romania, Bulgaria and, just before the First World War, Albania. In the Far East only China, because of its size, Japan, an island Empire, and Thailand, able to play off Britain against France, retained independence, while the European states encroached on both China and Thailand as they had previously done on Turkey and were to continue to do during the First World War.

Between 1914 and 1945 the world order continued to be dominated by European powers. Britain, France and Germany were separated from Russia (now the Soviet Union) by the 'Balkanisation' of Eastern Europe, where the Austrian and Turkish Empires had disappeared almost without trace. The rising power of the United States had come to dominate the western hemisphere, but its involvement in the First World War and its brief period of formal empire building (Hawaii, Samoa, Puerto Rico, the Philippines, the Canal Zone, the Virgin Islands) had ended and its withdrawal from world involvement had been accompanied by strong support for the dissolution of rival empires. Meanwhile, with the creation of the League of Nations, the first serious attempt had been made to constitute a new world order based on the formal equality of sovereign states, in which the former colonies of the European powers (Canada, Australia, India) would take their place by peaceful evolution.

The states that did not proceed directly to independence after the First World War were given a wholly new status. Despite the all-too evident desire of the governments of Britain and France to add them to their formal Empires, and their tendency afterwards to treat them as if they had in fact been so added, they were instead constituted as League of Nations Mandated Territories. In other words, they were to be administered by the victorious powers in such a way as to further their transition to independence at an early period. In the meanwhile, in the former Turkish territories of the Middle East in particular, Britain and France were able to retain control of a strategically sensitive area on the route to the Far East, but also to exploit the very considerable resources of oil that lay below the desert sands.

The considerable irony of treating these territories as ones which required a period of development prior to independence was not lost on either their rulers or their more educated citizens. Countries such as Iraq and Syria had been seats of advanced civilisation while Europe was in its infancy. Not only did they resent the assumption that they were not able to govern themselves, but in religious circles, particularly those surrounding the Mufti of Jerusalem in the British Mandated Territory of Palestine, there was a special resentment that the rule of Muslims had now passed into the hands of infidels. Religious leadership was, however, fragmented, following the secular revolution of Kemal Attatürk in Turkey itself, and the abolition of the Caliphate, on the one hand, and the rise of fundamentalist Islamic leadership under Ibn Saud on the other. Nationalist feeling also grew strong in the strategically key country of Egypt, which had already enjoyed relative independence in the early nineteenth century, and where a powerful historical symbolism was available for nationalist exploitation.

Despite the formal agreements embodied in the mandate system, the rivalry for influence between Britain and France was barely checked, and the antagonisms generated by the First World War alliance and its aftermath made it difficult for the two powers to act in common. The world order of the inter-war period, therefore, was much less stable than that of 1914, and efforts to re-establish the principle of balance of power in face of the rise of Hitler led only to the Second World War. Though both Britain and France appeared among the four victorious powers in 1945, France had been occupied and Britain humiliated in the Far East. By 1946–7 it became apparent that a new bipolar world order was emerging in which neither of the two new major powers, the United States and the Soviet Union, had any interest in conserving the old colonial empires.

In striking contrast with its predecessors, therefore, the new world order has been marked by the disintegration, not the development, of formal empires. At the same time, it is clear that each of the two superpowers have sought in this situation to add to their own spheres of influence, or, at the least, to deny new states to the sphere of their rival. They have, however, sought to do this in rather different ways.

The United States, faced with what it saw as a challenge

from the Soviet Union, responded by making use of the traditional instruments of diplomacy. Basic to the structure was a system of formal military alliances. The traditional claim of primacy within the western hemisphere, known as the Monroe Doctrine, was multilateralised by the creation of two organisations: a military alliance (the Rio Pact) and a regional organisation within the United Nations committed to applying on a regional basis the UN's mission of collective security, namely, the Organization of American States (OAS). In western Europe the formal alliance, the North Atlantic Treaty Organisation (NATO), had a consultative counterpart in the so-called Western European Union, but this failed to generate support, and was eventually to be superseded by the European initiative to create an Economic Community (1957) on a much narrower geographical basis. Outside these two areas the strategy of formal alliance was relatively unsuccessful; though by a direct alliance the United States took over directly the traditional links of Britain with Australia and New Zealand (ANZUS), alliance structures for south-east Asia foundered on local neutralism (SEATO) and initiatives for the Middle East created more trouble than they were worth, in view of the growing resentment at United States' suppport for Israel (MEDO/CENTO).

Outside this structure, the United States concluded a large number of bilateral military agreements. These formed one of two bases for the extensive use of aid programmes on a long-term basis, in a sense merely a natural extension of the wartime systems of military aid that had led up to and included Lend Lease. The other, the provision of economic aid for civilian development, was new. It began with the Marshall Plan, a successful initiative to restore the war-damaged industrial base of western Europe, from which, under Soviet prodding, the Eastern European countries that had at first been willing to participate, dissociated them-selves, as did the USSR itself. It was later to extend, in Latin America, Africa and south Asia, into a gigantic attempt to promote new industrial development and so to win friends among the new states.

The structures of aid and alliance were extended at the same time as the United States—as the world's largest

concentration of finance capital—had emerged by default
as the banker and creditor of the non-communist world.
By the later 1950s this was to give rise to increasing complaints among the new states that their position had not
really changed. When Ghana, for example, became independent in 1957 its leader, Kwame Nkrumah, who was initially
influenced by United States black consciousness and
Christian symbolism, adopted the saying 'Seek ye first the
political kingdom'. By the time of his deposition in 1966
he was already author of a sequel to Lenin, *Neocolonialism,
the Last Stage of Imperialism* (1965). Its theme, sounded also
by others, was that political independence was not enough,
for, to the visible control by colonialism, had succeeded an
invisible control of finance capital and dependence on market
prices set by the developed powers. The ultimate banker
of this system and largest consumer of raw materials, the
United States, thus became a 'neocolonialist' power. In the
late 1960s and 1970s the so-called 'dependency theorists'
were to carry this theme a stage further, arguing that by
maintaining the existing economic order the United States
and its developed client states were in fact actively promoting the underdevelopment of the Third World, that they
argued was a necessary condition of their own development
(Frank 1969, 1978, Cardoso and Faletto 1979). Aid and
investment, therefore, far from promoting the long-term
growth of the underdeveloped world, was actively seeking to
continue its state of deprivation. The two streams came
together in mid-decade in demands for a 'New International
Economic Order' from, in particular, the then Presidents of
Mexico and Venezuela on behalf of their colleagues of the
Third World (Arnell and Nygren 1980).

There were, of course, always public figures in the United
States prepared to argue that the formal structure of aid was
a denial of traditional American practice; that the structure
of private investment was as benign in its effects abroad as at
home. What was not always realised outside the United States
was that the government of that country, by the nature of
its political system, lacked any effective check on investment abroad. 'Neocolonialism', therefore, if it existed, was
not a system in the sense of being consciously guided and

directed. Hence, if it worked in favour of the United States, that was fortuitous, though certainly not unwelcome. The rising economic power of Japan, South Korea, Taiwan and Hong Kong certainly seemed to show that the dependency thesis—that the development of existing powers was incompatible with the development of latecomers—was quite incorrect.

The Soviet Union, as might have been expected from a country that had been invaded and had suffered badly from the ravages of the Second World War, initially took a very different attitude to the outside world, which it saw as fundamentally hostile territory. Only in Europe did it constitute a formal military alliance grouping, the Warsaw Pact, to match that of NATO. Far from receiving aid other than military, its members were required in many cases to pay reparations to the USSR itself, and their economic recovery was correspondingly delayed. This serious shortage of economic resources and its lack of productive capacity prevented it from developing an aid programme comparable to that of the United States, though in the 1950s it was to make a number of spectacular moves to enlist key support, notably by the agreement to finance the Aswan High Dam in Egypt in 1956 when western experts had doubted its value or desirability (cf. Feinberg 1983).

Having no stake in the existing diplomatic order, the Soviet Union returned to its traditional revolutionary posture in encouraging revolts in the colonial empires, for which purpose a new organisation, the Cominform, was constituted to replace the Comintern, which had been dissolved as a gesture of wartime solidarity with Russia's allies. It began with the advantage that in certain areas such revolts had already begun before the war's end, notably that in Indo-China against the French (the 'August Revolution', or First Indo-China War) and that in Indonesia against the Dutch. In the former case, Ho Chi Minh, a committed communist, was able, even with Chinese support, only to hold the northern part of Vietnam at the first peace settlement in 1954. The neutralist regimes of Sihanouk in Cambodia and of the Laotian princes, however, that emerged at the same time represented a useful strategic gain for the communists in the region and displayed much the same blend of nationalism, neutralism and self-conscious *rapprochement* with the USSR as did the regime of Sukarno in Indonesia or the self-consciously even-handed government of Pandit Nehru in India. By the late 1950s, therefore, the Soviet leaders had come not only to be received with respect in a much wider range of countries than had been the case with Stalin, but also in turn to recognise the validity of a 'non-aligned position', though this last they continued to regard as only a half-way stage to a committed socialist position recognising the Soviet Union as the leading anti-colonial force.

Between 1959 and 1961 the Soviet camp received the unexpected addition of support from Cuba. Because of its strategic value to the Soviet Union in the confrontation with the United States, this addition was welcomed, even though it proved very costly in continuing economic support. In due course it was admitted to formal alliance with the Soviet Union and became a member of Comecon. After this, and with increasing speed in the 1970s, a number of other newly-independent states, South Yemen, Somalia, Angola, Mozambique, Guiné e Cabo Verde, proclaimed themselves Marxist states and aligned themselves with the USSR without in the first instance the spur of an actual Soviet military presence or the close support of its assistance across a land frontier. Thus, the Soviet Union came to acquire an extended group of client states which looked to it for aid, which might, as in the case of Angola, involve open military assistance or, worse, as in the case of Somalia, be incompatible with support for a neighbouring Marxist regime, namely Ethiopia. In this way the Soviet Union began for the first time to incur the disadvantages that had previously been associated with the world-wide commitments of the United States, which, by a coincidence, was at the same time seeking, under the Nixon–Kissinger leadership, to withdraw from some of its more exposed positions. The immediate consequence of this last was the eventual victory in 1975 of communist forces in Cambodia and Laos as well as South Vietnam.

It must not necessarily be assumed that all national liberation movements in the post-1945 period necessarily involved one or other of the superpowers, even though it was generally believed at the time that this was the case. Events have since shown that the movements of the 1940s, then often attributed to 'communist infiltration', had in fact a strong nationalist content, and that attempts to transpose the methods used in one area, Vietnam for example, into others often proved unsuccessful. In the more recent period, the Third Indo-China War between Vietnam and China, the Ethiopia–Somalia contest for the Ogaden, and the Argentine attack on the Falkland Islands have all confirmed the primacy of nationalism over ideological affinities. The international system of the day has set some bounds for the pursuit of nationalism. The phenomenon itself remains varied and unpredictable.

THE PURSUIT OF NATIONAL IDENTITY

As we have already seen, the pursuit of political independence has been historically a prime objective of nationalists since the French Revolution. The concept of nation, it seems, has the same ability to legitimise in its supporters the willingness to resort to armed struggle as has religion, and, as in the case of the USSR itself in the Second World War bears witness, more power than that of the state. But how does such a struggle actually begin?

The first prerequisite is one of the three criteria for nationhood; linguistic, religious or cultural identity. The term 'ethnic' is often used, but is in practice hard to define meaningfully except in terms that admit a large proportion of the other criteria. Besides, there are cases such as that of Brazil in which it is clearly not at all appropriate.

What Anthony Smith calls the 'bearers' (Smith 1976, p. 21) of nationalism are therefore crucially important to its appearance, since it is necessary not only that these criteria exist in a given area, but that they come to be seen as important. Such individuals are characteristically of the intellectual elite, well-educated and with experience of life abroad that has thrown into relief for them their own sense of cultural separateness. Cultural identity, it seems, can only be realised in opposition to something else. At the same time, a sense of cultural identity does not preclude extensive borrowings from the dominant culture of the area, particularly where

such aspects are not seen at the time being as of crucial significance, or are invested with other desirable properties, for
example 'modernity'. In fact, a crucial factor in the emergence of leaders of independence movements seems, on the
contrary, to have been their access to higher education in the
metropolitan country; something shared by men otherwise as
disparate as Nehru, Nkrumah, Sukarno, and Dr Hastings
Banda.

The leader of an independence movement, in short, must
combine not only cultural identity but also proficiency in
the dominant culture which enables him to deploy it against
its proponents and gives him confidence to do so. In the post-
1945 period his claim to authority among his followers
was characteristically defined by the colonial authorities,
who sent him, as the British did Kenyatta or Makarios, into
detention or exile as an attempt to reduce his impact on the
nascent nationalist movement and to remove what was
essentially regarded as a focus of disaffection.

In an earlier period such leaders might have been less
fortunate. They themselves might have been executed, like
José Martí, and their followers suppressed by military force,
as by the Russian General who in 1830 reported 'La paix
règne à Varsovie' (Peace reigns in Warsaw). Attempts to
disengage national communist movements from Soviet
domination in eastern Europe in Hungary in 1956 and in
Czechoslovakia in 1968 were in similar fashion ruthlessly
suppressed by Soviet military power, and the Hungarian
leader, Imre Nagy, imprisoned and shot, as earlier were
nationalist resistance leaders in the Baltic States and the
Ukraine. On the other hand, the shooting of the leaders of
the Easter Rising in Dublin had exactly the effect of consolidating what had previously only been a weak national movement into a strong armed force, entirely alienated from the
sources of government authority; and democratic governments, such as that of Lloyd George in post-1918 Britain,
found public opinion unwilling to support long-term repressive measures of such a drastic nature. Such an option,
therefore, did not lie open to the post-1945 governments of
Britain, France, the Netherlands and Belgium.

A militant resistance movement, next, if it is to present an effective challenge, needs a source of arms. In the case of the post-1945 governments these came from the colonial powers themselves. They had been supplied, as in Burma, Malaysia and Indonesia, to use against the Japanese. The same was true in the first instances of the levies hastily raised to support the republic of Vietnam in 1945. Only later did it become possible for some of the enormous quantity of arms also supplied by the western powers to China to be redeployed secretly to aid the resistance struggle in south-east Asia. Western sources seem always to have underestimated the indigenous contribution to the success of such movements, and to have overestimated the amount of physical aid received from China and/or the Soviet Union. They were to do the same in the 1960s in evaluating the guerrilla movements in Latin America, a mistake shown even more recently in the Reagan administration's persistent belief, never convincingly documented, that the FMLN in El Salvador was receiving large arms shipments from Cuba via Nicaragua.

Lastly, once arms were available, an effective strategy had to be found for their use. Again, the indigenous importance of Truong Chinh (1963) in Vietnam, and even more notably the non-communist Nasution (1965) in Indonesia, is very clear. Nationalist movements have not in general operated to a grand strategic plan. Instead, they have relearned the lessons of war by trial and error, aided by two principal sources: recollections of their former past, as with Moshe Dayan in Israel, and the military manuals of the metropolitan forces themselves, as with the first Irish Republican Army.

Where they differed from internal revolutionary movements, as we have already seen, is that they did not necessarily have to achieve military victory. As the number of calls on the resources of the metropolitan states increased, it was sufficient to ensure that they were not themselves defeated. The case of Portugal presents only the most spectacular of the instances of the period in which growing war weariness caused a dramatic political reversal (*Sunday Times* 1975) leading to an agreed settlement; other examples being the agreement on the independence of Indo-China in 1954 and the Evian Agreement leading to the independence of Algeria in 1962. It is this combination of military and political strategies that has most strikingly been elaborated in the course of the period.

At the beginning of the period, there was strong public support for the United States for the war against the guerrillas in the Philippines and in Britain a series of colonial wars and in particular the 'Hola prison camp' scandal failed to become an issue in the 1959 General Election in Britain. In France, however, the fall of Dien Bien Phu brought about a drastic public reappraisal of the situation that had led its defender, General de Castris to allow his forces to become 'bottled up' without hope of escape, and enabled the Mendès-France government to cut French losses by withdrawal. The United States during the Vietnam War fell into the same trap of attempting to use traditional military strategy in a guerrilla war. The Nixon Administration, relying on much greater firepower than had been available to the French in 1954, tried to cut the Vietcong supply route (the 'Ho Chi Minh Trail') by strategic bombing, and extended the war to Cambodia in a vain attempt to achieve total denial. Despite protests the Administration was, however, able to retain adequate support based on its professions of peace-seeking at the negotiating table. It was only the Tet offensive of February 1972 that appeared to demonstrate the failure of this approach and hastened American withdrawal, and it is an irony that in military strategic terms the Tet offensive was in fact a severe defeat for the Vietcong and the North Vietnamese, while in political terms it was a decisive turning-point in their favour. For the simultaneous seizure of strong-points in many cities in South Vietnam led to a fierce counter-attack that cost the lives of many well-trained communist cadres without any hope of achieving the instant seizure of power. But, paradoxically, the fact that such a hopeless gesture could be attempted at all was taken in the United States as a sign of American weakness and destroyed all confidence in the ability of the South Vietnamese themselves to defend their own country. Thus, by closing the option of the Vietnamisation of the war, the Nixon Administration was left with no choice but to accept a humiliating withdrawal and the transfer of the Indo-Chinese territories to communist control.

How far this result was intended is very hard to assess. Fraternal support for the Vietcong had existed in the United States since the late 1960s, but remained always very marginal as an element in the United States peace movement. It is also probable that the North Vietnamese overestimated the strength of the peace movement as a whole, at least if they believed their own propaganda.

It is instructive to contrast the way in which for eleven years the Salazar government and its successor in Portugal managed, with only a tiny fraction of the resources available to the government of the United States, to sustain an anti-guerrilla campaign, not only in Angola, but also in Mozambique and Guiné. Control of the media and censorship of reports from the fighting zone minimised the effect of the fighting on public opinion, which in any case had no public expression in political form. The sole prominent political opponent of the regime within Portugal, Humberto Delgado, was secretly murdered on the Spanish frontier by the PIDE, the Portuguese Secret Police. World opinion, too, had only a minimal effect, as Portugal's NATO allies were unwilling to deny it the supplies of arms and ammunition needed to continue the campaign, for fear of a general communist take-over in southern Africa. It was, therefore, only among the armed forces of Portugal, where the true picture was known, that war weariness could be translated into political form, the result being the Revolution of 1975. Again, however, there seems no reason to suppose that this was for the insurgents a deliberately planned outcome, however welcome.

Once the colonial power (or equivalent) has withdrawn, as this last case shows, the consequences of wars of national liberation are by no means over. They have the effect of creating a distinctive style of political leadership in the new state which is the product of war, operates in a military mode and is particularly intolerant of internal opposition, which it regards, not as a valuable political discovery enabling a good government to maximise its political support, but as a colonialist encumbrance holding back national development. Where the struggle has been particularly fierce, opposition has been entirely eliminated; elsewhere it has been curtailed over time (Calvert 1976).

In the majority of cases the independent states have quickly adopted a presidential style of leadership, with the focus of power and public attention on a charismatic leader. Where there has been more than one such leader, as in Zimbabwe, the one who is in office at independence moves to eliminate his rival, as Robert Mugabe has done by sending the Fifth Brigade into the tribal lands of the supporters of Joshua Nkomo. There is a strong incentive for such leaders to become radicalised, since by doing so they avert any imputation that they were acceptable to the outgoing colonial government.

Such a style of leadership draws both on traditional sources in adopting, like Jomo Kenyatta, the emblems of traditional chieftainship, and on modern ones in attending the military parades and recalling the days of glory of the armed forces and their struggle. As the history of the Francophone African states in the early 1960s shows, all independent states are at first extremely vulnerable to military coups. Even the tiny army of ex-Dutch Surinam, only 300 strong, was able to seize control of the political system from the elected Prime Minister, Henck Arron, and slaughter both him and his supporters. But states that have already been militarised run in addition the extra risk of being involved in a major internal civil war, as disappointment grows at the actual outcome of independence and its inevitable failure to deliver all that the supporters of independence individually hoped from it. With much better communications, the new states have been far more successful in achieving speedy centralisation than their predecessors in Latin America, who spent much of the nineteenth century locked in a conflict between centralists and federalists. But there is every reason to suppose that the same pressures still exist, and account for the movements for regional autonomy or separatism that have been characteristic of India and the Philippines, to name but two very different examples.

A newly-independent state with a substantial military capability already in being, moreover, enters the international system not just as a client state but as an actor in its own right, capable of acting as a local or even regional power. It must therefore have regard not only to the global balance and its effect in its region, but on the internal dynamics of the situation in which it finds itself, and it is in any case going to be approached very soon to return the favours its neighbours may have done it in giving tacit or active support to its struggle for independence. Thus Nigeria, despite being itself torn by civil war and tribal conflicts leading to a demand for secession, could not but help becoming a focus for its African neighbours, and as an oil-rich state assuming a leadership role within the OAU. Zimbabwe, on the other hand, came to independence already locked into confrontation with South Africa, and, suffering from the depletion of civil war, was frustrated in its attempts to achieve the successful revolution of the whole of southern Africa that its leader may have dreamt of before independence. Like Mozambique, strong pressures have since operated to drive it back into alliance with the West, and certainly in Mozambique, only inept handling of the situation by the Reagan Administration in the United States seems for the time being at least to have cut the process short.

Lastly, successful nationalism coupled with military experience creates a strong demand for a command economy. Economies, however, do not necessarily respond well to command, and no government can put into the ground the mineral or energy resources that nature has failed to provide. The desire for economic independence, then, tends towards the creation of economies that replicate the features of existing ones, but in weaker form: the same emphasis on heavy industry, import substitution and control of what foreign investment may be permitted, but a weaker state to enforce such policies. It is this combination of weaknesses in face of the developed economies that has been the main burden of complaint of the proponents of the New International Economic Order, but the continuing political divisions that the situation embodies make it very unlikely that such a dramatic change could be achieved in the near future if at all.

4 The culture of violence

It is an important question whether there is, or is not, a pre-existing culture, or sub-culture, of violence in society, on which revolutionary movements draw. The fact that sociologists have spent much time discussing the nature of such a culture or sub-culture stems from its relevance to the practical tasks of administration presented by the existence of homicide and group violence. Both of these do, in some degree, relate to revolutionary activity, and the sociological evidence, which suggests that there are sharp differences between different societies in this regard, is therefore of considerable interest to any student of international relations.

Wolfgang and Ferracuti (1964) make use of the United Nations' statistics on the rate of homicide in different societies. On the figures presented, Mexico ranks top, and Colombia second. Both are countries in which revolutionary activity has historically been important; in Mexico during the period of the Mexican Revolution, and in Colombia during the period of the *Violencia* in the late 1940s and early 1950s. On the same figures, the United States ranks very high, but, perhaps significantly, not as high relative to Europe as is often thought. The general rate of homicide and violence in the United States bears reasonable comparison with those for certain other European countries, the more spectacular newspaper comparisons usually being made with the urban figures for the United States, for example those for New York and Chicago. The example of the United States, therefore, does not necessarily disprove the relationship between a high level of violence and the incidence of revolution. But in any case this is not necessarily the point at which we should be looking. The question is not whether they are directly related, as political scientists have tended to assume, but whether the existence of group violence lends a particular range of possibilities to potential revolutionary movements.

Group violence is used as a general indicator of political *malaise* (Russett 1964, p. 73) and has been examined in detail by sociological writers. In the wake of the assassination of President Kennedy there was much detailed study of the relationship between group violence and political action in the United States, and the National Commission on Violence (Kirkham *et al.* 1970) showed that 'the level of assassination corresponds to the level of political turmoil and violence in general' (p. 294). They based this generalisation on a study of a number of other countries, statistically analysed. Moreover, 'in comparison to other nations, the United States experiences a high level of political violence and assassination attempts (ibid., p. 294). This suggests that the comparison with revolutionary behaviour has to be regarded with some suspicion, since the United States is not generally considered to be a strongly revolutionary nation. They also observed the widespread existence of vigilantism in the United States. They observed that historically such spontaneous quasi-legal behaviour by citizens was related to 'the right of revolution' reiterated, for example, by Engels. But in the American context it appeared to be less related to the right of revolution in view of its low relationship with what it termed to be revolutionary violence in United States values, and its high relationship to the persistence of individualism generally in American society, a factor which is undoubtedly unusual among world societies and not to be taken as typical.

There are two principal comments that can be made on the report of the National Commission. First of all, there have to be considerable reservations with regard to the gross figures on which it is based. In Mexico, for example, physical violence is strongly and positively equated with masculinity and toughness. It is not, therefore, regarded as socially unacceptable (Stevens 1974). And in the modern period violence in Mexico has been characteristically individual, as compared notably with Colombia, where its high level, like that in Northern Ireland, reflects the major feuds between contending parties (Fals Borda 1965). So the nature of violence, as between individual and group violence, therefore needs to be clearly distinguished.

Secondly, there has to be considerable reservation about the actual reporting of figures. In Mexico, where violence is not disapproved of socially, there appears to be relatively little impediment to its reporting, and it has to be presumed that the government of Mexico is not unwilling to let these figures be generally known. In practice, however, most countries simply do not report such figures, or, if they do, include them in a general reserve category where their significance is lost. Conversely, in some societies there may be considerable reluctance to report as, for example, with the proverbial low rate of suicide in the Irish Republic, where the Catholic Church disapproves strongly of it. It is therefore necessary, it seems, to qualify one's assessment of the incidence of violence within society with some other indicator which is more easily generalised. A significant one, probably, is the use of force by government, given the interactive nature of the revolutionary process. Government use of force is much more widely reported, and much less amenable to suppression than generalised statistics on individual violence drawn over a large area, but it does present its own particular problems and, again, governments may be unwilling to have such data made publicly available.

The significance of the use of force by government is in the first instance the evidence it presents about the role of violence in the dominant culture. The dominant culture is the official culture of the rulers of the society, in relation to which, in Marxist terms, the cultures of other subordinate classes are formed. Such cultures can, therefore, only be fully understood in relation to the dominant culture. In turn, the formation of subcultures stems from the impact of the dominant culture on its rivals as it changes according to the socio-economic conditions of the time. The fact that the rulers are willing freely to make use of force to maintain their own position is a major factor favouring the easy acceptance of violence by other elements within society, and it is inevitable that to some subcultures at least, identity will be sought in the deployment of violence against the holders or symbols of an authority that is regarded as being repressive. In many Latin American societies violence is characteristically used most of all by governments.

As Duff and McCamant (1976) show, the continued use of force by governments reduces social cohesion when, as so often happens, it acts arbitrarily to ensure that the 'rules of the game' fail to establish themselves in such a way that its effective authority is limited. Such rules of the game act to reduce and channel the number of demands, forcible or otherwise, that a government has to confront at any one time.

Dissident individuals, as such, present little threat to government except in the rare case of political assassinations, and the more successfully a government operates a system of justice that caters for the demands of individuals, the less likely it is that they will aggregate sufficiently to become a threat. Threats to governments, therefore, come from groups, and the three most significant forms of group threat may be conveniently subdivided as gang behaviour, social banditry, terrorism and external attack, the last of which has already been dealt with in Chapter 2 above.

GANGS

Gang behaviour, especially in the young and adolescent, is generally seen as normal in human societies, and even as functional. Gang behaviour, for example, lies at the basis of most courtship rituals. As with other human behaviour, integration into the gang involves the management of aggression (Lorenz 1966, Tiger 1969, Morris, 1969).

Lorenz regards such management as being the control of a 'failsafe' mechanism to protect the group against sudden attack, and therefore basic to the existence of the group. Its management normally, he suggests, involves externalisation on fixed objects, whether another gang or an individual.

There is of course considerable doubt as to whether aggression is in fact 'normal' in the human condition, whatever that may mean. And, indeed, many progressive thinkers are unwilling to accept that it may be. However, it seems fairly generally agreed that such behaviour, aggressive behaviour, is of particular significance in human societies which have become urbanised. A good deal of literature exists on this aspect, for the understanding of which it is not necessary to have held very strong views one way or the other on the basic function of aggression in human societies.

It seems that there are several possible responses to the existence of aggression in urbanised societies. The most obvious is the acceptance of it as a normal incident of civilisation, a degree, if you like, of 'normal neurosis' (Putney and Putney 1964). Empirically, it appears that there is an irreducible minimum of violence which cannot be totally eliminated, at least in the present state of our knowledge of human society, and therefore a degree of acceptance, though it may not much help those involved in the violence, will at least keep the rest of us happy.

The second response is the therapy of the individual, and the satisfaction by this of individual needs. Perls, a *Gestalt* therapist, has suggested that the urge to violence within urbanised society results from an absence of normal outlets for aggression, which he sees as being related to the natural need to bite and savage prey in search of food (Perls 1969). Although such a view lends itself to parody, it does suggest useful lines of research based, possibly, on the nature of food consumed in given societies and the degree to which other forms of aggressive behaviour are in fact socially acceptable.

A third response is the somewhat pessimistic concern about the future of an increasingly urbanised society (Mass Society) by sociologists who expect 'meaningless' violent behaviour to increase. Therapy here is seen as being essentially aimed at the group rather than at the individual, but since it takes the form of the individualisation of society, by the promotion of community action groups and other small organisations designed to satisfy individual needs, it may well have a more direct application. Curiously enough, this view relates closely to the preceeding one, in that it appears that the gang behaviour which is characteristically disruptive within urban societies is in fact a spontaneous attempt to satisfy this need for smaller groups for associational purposes.

Specifically, pessimism about such development stems from the belief that such societies are characteristically a prey to mass movements led by demagogues of potentially revolutionary sympathies (Chakotin 1940, p. 38). Here the cry is for defence, rather than for therapy, though once again it takes the form of individual alertness and awareness. Such mass movements have been seen by their hostile critics as being virtually 'political gangs' and their relationship to the study of gang behaviour is therefore of particular interest.

Sociological study of gangs, however, does not suggest that they form an important reservoir of violence available to be tapped by revolutionaries. On the contrary, gangs represent in the main the development among predominantly working-class youth of a sub-culture within which they can be at home, and from which they can withstand something of the pressures to which they are otherwise exposed from the dominant culture. They are, moreover, highly localised, being rooted in the local communities of which they form part, and are conditioned to a temporary and cyclical existence by the relentless pressure of the need to conform to the working week. They do not, in short, exist independently of the structure of society as they find it, and economic necessity ensures that they cannot do so. Their aggression, where it exists significantly, is focused on rival gangs rather than on the structure of authority in the state as a whole (Hall and Jefferson 1977).

Adult gangs are not very different. Their endurance does involve political awareness and organisation to a level that ensures that they assert themselves in the political management of the communities of which they form part. Failing that, they are no more durable. Al Capone was apprehended in the end not for murder or robbery, but for tax evasion. Such organisations, however, far from being revolutionary in effect, have a particularly strong influence on maintaining the existing order of society, for it is by its maintenance that they can alone hope to survive and to make money.

As will be seen, it has been the view of most studies of gang behaviour carried out for sociological purposes that groups are, in effect, from a political point of view, virtually proto-political communities, which substitute for remote and/or inaccessible authorities (Fromm 1960). This view is so widely held that it comes as some surprise to discover that there are exceptions. A significant one, however, is provided by Yablonsky, who in his study of the so-called violent gang demonstrates that it is in fact almost totally asocial. Moreover, the violence associated with it is in fact mostly talk, as the members of it are so asocial that they lack both the organisation and the ability to co-operate in order to organise successful combat (Yablonsky 1962). The element of organisation, therefore, is obviously intrinsic to political, as opposed to purely asocial behaviour, and it is precisely this element which in the past has received so little attention.

BANDITRY

When we turn to the subject of banditry, however, we find that we are in the presence of a different phenomenon. To start with, banditry is essentially a rural activity, and its relationship to behaviour in modern urbanised societies is still uncertain. Hobsbawm (1972) shows that, far from being just criminals, alienated anti-social elements, the bandits of the past, operating in rural communities, were a defined professional group. This thesis seems to be well supported by the evidence and to be entirely acceptable. He goes beyond this, however, to talk about what he calls the 'social bandit', motivated not just by loot but by desire for social justice. Of these he identifies three types:

1. The *noble robber* or 'Robin Hood'. His characteristic is that he robs the rich to give to the poor. It is, of course, true that most bandits prefer to rob the rich since they have more money, but undeniably many of them do not choose to give their money to the poor, so we may accept this as a defined type.
2. The *haiduks*. These are primitive resistance fighters or organised guerrillas, and they have a characteristically political motivation, being primitive only in the sense that they are operating in under-developed societies in which banditry is a natural form of self expression.
3. The terror-bringing *avenger*. He exists in the public consciousness because he rights by his own form of instant justice wrongs which society is either powerless or unwilling to right.

As ideal types, these three are useful, though it must be observed that they do in fact overlap, and that a primitive resistance fighter such as Pancho Villa springs into prominence first when he acts to avenge a wrong, in this case, traditionally, the rape of his sister, and gains in his later years a reputation for generosity and openhandedness which is the hallmark of a noble robber. In other words, the ideal types presented by Hobsbawm must be seen as overlapping categories, each of them of some significance in limiting the political appeal of a specified actor.

It appears, however, that the particular form of political action taken will depend on a number of things, of which the most important is no doubt the individual's own make-up and capacity. But banditry as a general social phenomenon is another matter entirely. The practice of banditry is aided specifically by geographical remoteness and the absence of roads, particularly those open to governmental forces. But it is more specifically related to a type of political remoteness, especially where jurisdictions are complex, badly delimited, or the subject of competition between states. In feudal society a bandit can easily become the founder of government, and indeed of a whole state. In modern times, Hobsbawm holds, the social bandit has disappeared. But he has not disappeared completely; he has instead been replaced by peasant guerrilla leaders such as those of the movements described in Wolf (1970) in Mexico, Russia, China, Vietnam, Algeria and Cuba. In modern times the guerrilla leader has, therefore, taken over many of the characteristics of the bandit and, it may be presumed, something of the same mystique and political support. But, significantly, banditry does not transplant to the cities, where the characteristic feature of political action is terrorism.

TERRORISM

Terrorism, a phenomenon common in modern urban societies, is regarded by most dwellers within such societies with abhorrence, though the majority of them are unwilling to risk themselves personally by expressing this abhorrence openly. A small group of people, normally active in it, approve of terrorism as a possible cleansing influence in a society which they see as being hopelessly out of control. And it may well be that others than Hyams (1975) can take a longer perspective in regarding it as a 'cathartic fever incident to civilisation' (Hyams, p. 189). Terrorism is capable of description, delimitation, and even classification (Wilkinson 1974). It seems to be less easily capable of control, but this still has to be proved (cf. Wilkinson 1978).

Wilkinson sees the close relationship between government and opposition as lying at the root of his classification of terrorism, for which he has three categories. These are revolutionary terrorism, sub-revolutionary terrorism, and repressive terrorism. Of these, the second and third categories relate to the government and opposition respectively; the first, however, is a more complex phenomenon embracing both. And it is significant that it is extremely difficult to draw a clear boundary line in any given set of circumstances between the use of one, and the use of the other, for the two do seem indeed to be so closely related that they cannot be separated. Wilkinson deals with a number of different situations in which terrorism is used. Assassination of the unworthy, often for religious or semi-religious motives, closely relates to Hobsbawm's category of the avenger. That of terror against indigenous autocracy, a purely political phenomenon, reminds us of the non-existence within these societies of any organised opposition of any other form, which is capable of expressing itself within any non-violent political process. The third category of liberation from foreign rule directs our attention outwards beyond the confines of the state and has not so far been the subject of this discussion. Here it shades off into sub-revolutionary terrorism at the international level.

The bulk of Wilkinson's discussion is concerned with the use of terrorism in two other circumstances, each of which is purely political in character. The first is resistance to totalitarian societies, the second the use of terror against the liberal democracies in order to undermine them and subject them to totalitarian rule. Both are opposite sides of the same coin. And the question that it seems that it is useful to pursue here is not the question of how terrorism is used in these circumstances but why terrorism should become to be used as a weapon at all. Here it seems particularly important to devote attention to the psychological origins of the individual, for the psychological origins of terrorist action seem to be in general terms those common to agitators, namely the displacement of private motives into public life

(Lasswell 1960). Specifically, it lies in what Erikson (1968) describes as the rejection of negative identities ('images of self') and their elimination from other social groups in which they appear. Since this involves the actual killing of individuals, it is necessary for the psychological stability of the individual to redesignate the members of such social groups as sub-human, a process which Erikson calls their designation as a 'pseudo-species'. But this in turn can only be supported in the individual by an elaborate psychological mechanism designed to prevent the breakdown of his own identity in the face of actions which he has been instinctively taught to believe from an early age to be essentially barbarous.

The question is, however, has he in fact been taught to consider them barbarous, or has the society in which he lives allowed him to perform such acts? This is where banditry, as a noble career, appears such an attractive vehicle for the revolutionary, and yet there is little or no evidence that such banditry has in fact ever served a major revolutionary purpose. In the most spectacular case of Northern Mexico during the Revolution, it is not the bandit who in fact succeeded in promoting revolutionary changes, political, social, or economic, which ultimately form the political significance of the revolution (Wilkie and Wilkie 1970). The urban terrorist, on the other hand, appears to serve no useful social purpose beyond pulling down the fabric of society for others to build in its place. It is hard to think of any major terrorist who has in fact become the successful leader of a political movement, in the sense that such leaders, if they become political leaders, appear normally to have been those who have not themselves personally taken part in political action. The successful general does not risk his own precious life in the cause, he leaves that to others. (And they, in turn, are bound to be disappointed with the results which he negotiates on their behalf.)

Terrorist methods, however, as we have already noted, have frequently been employed in the course of movements of national liberation. It is such movements, therefore, that offer the most striking examples of the importance of education in the perpetuation of political stability—or instability. Undoubtedly, great national heroes may serve as powerful examples in a unified political culture for the maintenance of that culture. Yet the very different examples of Belgium and Northern Ireland remind us that even the peaceful perpetuation of ethnic or religious rivalries, far from contributing to the maintenance of a peaceful society, may constantly act to frustrate it. In such cases, the existence of the dominant culture is constantly under challenge, but its strength of example ensures the survival of opposition in a form sufficiently effective to keep it constantly on the defensive. The maintenance of separate schools (Ireland) or political parties (Netherlands) as training grounds for the 'bearers' of identity is particularly important. Here too we find that the cycle of violence and repression acts permanently to renew the effect of examples instilled by the process of education. The tree of liberty is refreshed constantly by the blood of fresh martyrs, and individuals recruited to the political cause do not, therefore, need a separate identity from that of the group; the roles are already written for them to play.

Obviously there would be a considerable advantage to a revolutionary movement to be able to recruit to its cause groups of followers already skilled in the art of fighting and so to short-circuit the long process of building up their strength. With the recruitment of individuals, both as leaders and supporters, I propose to deal in detail in the next chapter (Chapter 5). As regards groups, however, there does not appear to be much evidence that this is the case. Rather, a revolutionary movement tends to draw for its support on politicised groups who then subsequently turn to violence to achieve their ends. Whether they do so or not, of course, depends not only on the existence of such groups with effective leadership, but on two other factors: whether the nature of their political goals are such that violence appears to be a plausible option for achieving them, and whether or not the material facilities (e.g. weapons) can be obtained or made available to them at crucial points in the political action.

Given these two conditions, even individuals may be able to effect major changes in the political process. There is probably no aspect of the definition of revolutionary change in terms of the use of force that has raised more criticism than the implication that in certain circumstances political assassination may have 'revolutionary' consequences. For this implies that such political assassinations are in fact 'revolutionary events', and it is one of the universally accepted 'facts' about politics that assassinations are the work of individual, demented persons acting without political motivation and so have no possible political significance. Yet, as the National Commission report reminds us, this does not appear in fact to be the case. Only in one of the assassinations of United States' Presidents does the political motivation appear to be absent, and the evidence from other countries supports the view that, on the contrary, political assassination is in fact highly significant as an indicator of growing political stress. The point is that political assassins who act on their own, without the protection afforded by a revolutionary party or terrorist group, seldom fail to escape capture and, in consequence, execution. They cannot therefore contribute subsequently to the growth of the revolutionary movement which, as in Egypt in 1948, or Panama in 1955, their action may have acted to foreshadow (see also Havens, Leiden and Schmitt 1970).

Groups which can be recruited *en bloc* to support revolutionary movements may be expected, therefore, to have two characteristics: a preparedness to use force in the pursuit of political objectives, and the material facilities to do so. Two groups present in almost all societies possess both these attributes, the military and the police. Indeed, the nature of the calling of each of these means that, particularly when acting together (as frequently happens) they are most likely to get their way. The special role of the military will be discussed further in Chapter 6. Here it is only necessary to point out that to understand the particular circumstances in which the military, as in Egypt in 1952 and in Peru in 1968, act as a radically transforming social force, it is first necessary to understand the way in which they achieve power, and this requires us inevitably to consider the much larger number of cases in which the military use their capacity for armed intervention in politics to forestall or to arrest the possibility of social revolution.

The existence of a powerful military force in society, if coupled with a draft or selective service system for adult males, has the added effect of spreading military skills more widely within the civilian population. Unfortunately, it is not at all easy to determine how far, if at all, this contributes to the spread of revolution. It is probably true that at most times in most societies, the wide distribution of military skills has acted to promote political violence. Since 1787 in the United States, it has been enshrined in the Second Amendment to the American Constitution, that it should, properly organised, achieve the exact reverse: that the existence of a well-regulated militia force is an essential guarantee of popular liberty.

This view did not originate in the United States. Switzerland is the first country that comes to mind for most people in which the creation of a 'citizen army' has acted not only as an effective protection against external attack but also as a barrier to the ambitions of local politicians. Certainly the history of that country since 1848 would seem to bear that view out. But reference to its earlier history would suggest a modification of that view which in no way supports the views of the American National Rifle Association or those Americans who consider that in arming themselves to the teeth they are helping to keep the communist menace at bay. In the eighteenth century the sturdy independence of Switzerland made it, not the United States, but the Cuba of its day—a place where revolutionaries could find refuge the revolutionary ideas were published and traded in in a way that infuriated its larger neighbours. Indeed, without the revolutionary ferment in Switzerland at that time, the onset of the French Revolution of 1789 might well have been delayed, and the dramatic effect of the writings of the Genevese Jean-Jacques Rousseau could scarcely be imagined if he had not had living examples of the things he talked about to back his own philosophical self-assurance.

In any case, the nature of weaponry has changed so much, especially since 1945, that it is now very difficult to see how even the best-trained citizen army could resist the determined use of force by its own government, if for some reason (e.g. defeat in war) that government's capacity for force were to escape from the control of its own citizens. It is not merely the possession of weapons, but the ability to deploy and use them effectively that is at issue, and to restrain the ordinary use of firearms, etc., in crime, modern governments have in recent years acquired a quite extraordinary degree of technical skill. Thus, as a restraint on the spread of weapons, there has been the ability to check for their presence at airports, etc.; to the development of plastic explosives, improved devices for defusing or disposing of bombs and so on.

As is widely recognised, much of the effectiveness of terrorist techniques in promoting the spread of and confidence in revolutionary ideas in the late 1960s and early 70s stemmed, not from the nature of the acts themselves, but from their role in the 'theatre of violence'. Liberal democratic societies seemed particularly vulnerable to such challenges because of the way in which the existence of a free press and open access to radio and television enabled terrorists to 'orchestrate' their efforts to maximum effect, making use, in fact, of the reactions of uncommitted citizens to put pressure on their governments in a way that the relatively tiny terrorist groups could never in themselves have hoped to do.

In societies with a strong authoritarian tradition, such as Turkey or Guatemala, the ability to take strongly repressive measures unhampered by democratic inhibitions appeared to their governments at one time to be highly effective. Not only could control of the media be used to minimise the theatrical effect of terrorist violence, but governmental counter-terror could proceed unchecked by criticism from within. What was not appreciated was the extent to which the decision of a government to resort to unchecked terror against its own people would, by destroying the internalised norms that check social violence in the individual, create a dangerously unstable situation with an endless potential for the escalation of violence. No government has ever succeeded in the past in eliminating entirely all challenges to its authority, nor does the development of technology—despite the extent to which it does offer governments a range of abilities not previously available—stop short of national frontiers. Consequently, just as the possibility of the total control of information seemed on the verge of being achieved, the development of the transistor radio, the increase in demand for world travel and the development of the means of reproducing the printed word, combined to put it once again out of reach.

It is, therefore, with the development of such internalised norms that a society seeking real long-term stability must be concerned, and this, inevitably, means the development of education. Just as, during the Vietnam War, the sight for the first time in the history of warfare of actual battlefield conditions in the homes of ordinary American citizens, was by far the most powerful force in bringing about disillusion with the effectiveness of military action in the international context, so the reporting of the civil war in El Salvador has consistently undercut the Reagan Administration's persistent assertion that a purely military solution to that conflict was both necessary and desirable (cf. Pearce 1981). On the other hand, the actual presence of such sights in El Salvador itself clearly does not have the same effect on those who are already committed to the victory of one side or the other. There, whatever native inhibitions on killing they may have begun with or been educated in, have long since been overlaid by the conditioning of more recent experiences. It is clearly of crucial importance that a better understanding of the social and psychological mechanisms involved be both developed and imparted to the next generation of citizens, but there can be no great optimism that this will in fact be done.

5 Leadership and recruitment

Eric Hoffer, in *The True Believer* (Hoffer 1951, pp. 129 ff.) says that revolutions need three types of men: men of words, fanatics, and men of action. By which he means that men of words are required to make people aware of the deficiencies in their existing political condition, to alert them to the deficiencies of the existing social order. Fanatics are required to risk the consequences of actually attacking the existing social order and bringing it down. To reshape it they need to be single-minded, dedicated men who are prepared to tear away at history with their bare hands. But men of action are also required, to reconstruct. Revolution for Hoffer, as for most modern writers, is not simply a question of tearing down; it is a question of re-shaping, re-building, building up.

Hoffer is talking, in fact, about the element of leadership. He does not imply that revolutions are made *solely* by means of words, fanatics and men of action. He is talking about the leadership of revolution. It is true that revolution is not practicable without the mobilisation of a considerable body of men and women. But the fact is that some kind of direction, some kind of organisation is required; even if it is collective leadership, it is nevertheless a form of leadership. Leadership in revolutions, therefore, not only *may* be plural; it frequently *is* plural. Revolutions are not, as was at one time believed, merely the product of a single, individual motivation. Unless the individual leader, whatever his psychological drives, calls up some kind of response in a body of supporters, he cannot become a revolutionary leader, or indeed a political leader of any kind.

There are special problems in the study of revolutionary leadership, such as those raised by the necessity for concealment or for surreptitious action. This means that sometimes people who appear to be the leaders are not necessarily in fact the true ones; and this is a problem—a practical problem of research. In addition, most of what has been written on this subject in the past has been rather conditioned by the authors' own social backgrounds and interests. With both these points in mind, I propose to deal first of all with the social origins of revolutionary leadership, and then with the psychological ones.

THE SOCIAL ORIGINS OF LEADERSHIP

Pettee (1938) suggested that the origins of the revolutionary impulse lay in the realisation of 'cramp'—a peculiar word which we would now probably render rather more happily as 'frustration'. 'Cramp', for Pettee, is the realisation that one is not able to achieve what one would like to achieve, that one is restricted in one's possibilities. What then determines the revolutionary's response, it appears, is his class or ethnic or other origins. As Brinton has pointed out, the leaders of great revolutions often come from the second social rank and they step into the political vacuum left by the overthrow of the existing government (Brinton 1952; Calvert 1970b).

Even in military coups one discerns repeatedly the problem of the blockage of promotion. It is true that commanders-in-chief of armies frequently lead military coups but it is equally true that many other leaders of coups are people of a superior rank somewhere below the top; in other words they feel that they are aspiring to something beyond this. The self-promotion of colonels, as in Egypt and Libya—and indeed even in the case of Cuba, majors—confirms that there are similar social pressures operating at lower military levels also, but that officers at this level are more prone to develop radical views. It is often suggested that revolutionary leaders emerge simply from personal frustration. The biggest possible argument against this is that a great many people spend most of their working lives being frustrated, in terms of promotion. And yet most people never become revolutionary leaders. One must account, in other words, not just for the leadership element, but also for the revolutionary element. Many approaches to revolutionary leadership are misleading because they have concentrated in the first instance on the fact of revolution, and have tended to neglect the organisational aspects which are as important in revolution as in anything else.

For example, the career of Napoleon has been held out for many years as an example of the '*carrière ouverte aux talents*' —in other words that the French Revolution offered him an opportunity to rise to the top in a way he would not otherwise have been able to do. This is very questionable. Napoleon was already in the French army by 1789 and furthermore he had already gone through military college and was already an officer by 1789, which suggests that he was not that much blocked, and given his age at the time (thirty) he had the seniority one would have expected at that age. What the French Revolution gave him was the opportunity to shine in war. In other words, the French government—be it royalist or revolutionary (we must remember that the war started while it was still royalist)—embarked on a policy of military conquest which, such was the surprise of all the other states in Europe, was unusually successful; and because it was unusually successful, the opportunities for military promotion were extremely rapid, and there was, because of the decapitation of the state—in this case quite literally— therefore no limit to the possibilities to which an ambitious general with military talent could rise.

The second point to remember about Napoleon, is that he was an exponent of the new and important art of artillery. He was an artillery officer; he was not an infantry officer, still less a cavalry officer, and this played a major part in his rapid rise. Artillery was the key to success in war at this time, and he was an able exponent of what was needed in the circumstances.

On the other hand, as evidence of his uniqueness, it has been pointed out that he was Corsican by origin. Corsica, formerly Italian, had only very shortly before become part of French territory, making him a French citizen. This is true, but Cardinal Mazarin, who was ruler of France in all but name from 1643 to 1660, was also Italian by birth, and he attained his position, a century and more before Napoleon, by a completely different kind of promotional ladder and one which had nothing to do with revolution. So this suggests that having Italian origin was not an obstacle to holding power in pre-Revolutionary France and therefore the fact of Napoleon's success in post-Revolutionary France is not necessarily a recommendation for revolution as a vehicle for promotion.

It was not necessary to be unprincipled, or even non-principled like Talleyrand, whose sole principle was to survive, in order to work for the French Revolution. Men of ideals did in fact find the old regime stifling. They spent a great number of years explaining why, but not just because it was stifling them. What, after all, could a Rousseau reasonably complain about a France which lionised him, fêted him, gave him every sign of respect, distinction, talked about his books all the time, raised him to consideration in the salons of the great, and so forth? But the fact is that he had the capacity which many other writers have had, to realise the weaknesses in the situation for other people and the potential social consequences of these weaknesses. 'Man is born free but everywhere he is in chains', he wrote, and yet he did manage to find somewhere reasonably tolerable to live himself (McDonald 1965). On the other hand, the writers who expounded these idealistic critiques of French society before the French Revolution were not the people who directed it. The Abbé Sièyes is the only writer of any consequence to have played a major role in the French Revolution and he was soon to seek exile. Condorcet, on the other hand, was actually executed after a long imprisonment in the Temple, in which he managed to realise only the first part of his masterwork—what was to be his masterwork—a sketch of human progress from the beginning up to the time of the French Revolution, in eight parts. The men of words only provided the preconditions for the French Revolution.

The works of Robespierre and Danton show us the revolutionaries in action, but one has to remember that they are not works in the conventional sense. What Robespierre said was said at the rostrum in the assembly, or on the occasion of one of the great festivals of the French state. Robespierre's interpretation of Rousseauism as a revolutionary ideology is an *ad hoc* interpretation. He is busy expounding in the circumstances of the moment, in the heat of the moment; he is expounding what he feels people ought to do next, and why they ought to do it. Therefore he is one of the fanatics rather than one of the men of words, the men who reduce all problems to the simple question of disposing of the government.

Sweep away the vestiges of the past, such men argued, government included, and the new order will emerge. All that is lacking, they suggested, is that these restraining conditions should be swept away, and then liberty, equality, fraternity would reign. The degree of idealism in this viewpoint is hard to assess because it is so much constrained by the obvious over-simplification of the problems of human nature, the problems of living in societies. Societies have not got any simpler since 1789; they tend on the whole to have become rather more complicated.

The third point is that one of the problems with interpreting the role of leadership in revolution is the fact that when one does interpret it one normally goes straight for the most complex definition of revolution. One looks at the great revolutions and thinks: what kind of leadership was required firstly, to bring down the old regime; secondly, to destroy the vestiges of fuedalism; thirdly, to create the new French state; fourthly, to establish a new social order. We tend to look at them altogether. Whereas in fact these are of course disparate problems, and with a different kind of leadership for each, even though there is an institutional continuity between these forms of leadership. If we go back to the root meaning of revolution and think of it basically as an act of applied aggression (though not simply as an act of applied aggression), then it is rather easier to see why it becomes, as such, a relatively neutral vehicle which allows the acting out of various kinds of impulses arising from diverse social causes.

It is even rather questionable whether there is any clear class interest. One has to remember that even Marx had to allow for the fact that the proletariat may not be aware— and indeed in his day was not aware—of their role in the scenario for the future that he was writing, that they would have to be instructed and guided. One of the basic problems that Marxists have never been able to agree on, not even within any one trend or persuasion of Marxism, is the precise role of the communist party. This is frequently flannelled over by saying the party is after all the force that directs and guides the revolution. But what if, as in Cuba, for example, the party is not created until two years after the seizure of power has actually been consummated? Some Cubans then suggested that the party somehow, retrospectively, guided the Cuban revolution (Goldenberg 1965). This is a view that they have now dropped. They just accept that the party now guides the destinies of the state, without explaining exactly how the party came to exist. But it is a real difficulty, especially with the Leninist persuasion of Marxism, which of course attributes key significance to the 'leading role' of the party.

Of course there are obvious reasons why one should wish, in the Russian context, to emphasise the direction of the party. The party in Russia was a minority interest which was seizing control of the revolution, directing it much more rapidly on its course than anyone could have previously anticipated, and telescoping the 'bourgeois' and the 'proletarian' revolutions. Moreover, Marx expected some kind of alliance between the proletariat and the most 'advanced' section of the bourgeoisie, the revolutionary intelligentsia, which would have otherwise no clear class interest as such. If the intelligentsia is going to guide and then direct the proletariat of which it does not form a part, it must be because it realises that this is what the trend of history indicates it will do, and not because it has common class interests as such.

However, as I have shown elsewhere, under any of the definitions of class that are widely accepted, there remains a conflict between class interests and class origins. Class origins of people who take part in revolutions, the evidence suggests, tend to conform to the general distribution of classes within society—in other words, people who take part in revolutions are much like people who take part in any other kind of politics; they take part in rough proportion to the social origins of people within society, as we shall see later.

Similarly, the displacement of class by class is not a displacement of a complete set of individuals by another complete set of individuals of different class origin. It was

Lenin who first attempted to redefine revolution as a displacement of one class by another class, not Marx. Marx himself
spent a long time discussing events as revolutions, that are
not, in fact, displacements of class by class, and never
pretended to be. But in considering the Leninist interpretation of Marxism, one must remember, therefore, that when
he says 'displacement of class by class' he is talking about
control, not composition. In fact, even after the Russian
Revolution a substantial number of people remained in
government who in fact had been there before.

The question of to what extent the control in any given
revolution is absolutely transferred from one side to the
other remains one of the very interesting enigmas of history.
And of course it does raise the question that, if there are
bourgeois survivors in a post-revolutionary state in Russia,
then is it because in fact no complete displacement took
place? Or is it purely due to the fact that the city tends to
bourgeoisify the people who live in it?

THE PSYCHOLOGICAL ORIGINS OF LEADERSHIP

Biographies of revolutionary leaders tend to assume some kind
of psychological motivation, but this is often still at a very
simplistic level. E. V. Wolfenstein (1967), for example, who
makes use of a Freudian scheme, emerges at the end with
the conclusion that the qualities of the leaders he studies
are ruthlessness, dogmatism and self-determination, flexi-
bility, toughness and sound administrative ability. The
conclusion, it seems to me, is not tremendously rewarding,
except in the point about sound administrative ability.
Looking at revolutionary leadership, the people who stand out
are in fact those people who were able to administer; in other
words, they were politicians and people who were able to run
a system which they had created. And they were, incidentally,
people who had also learnt the trick of changing the rules so
that they played the game the way they wanted to.

The development of modern psychology is very accurately
reflected in the development of psychological theories of the
origins of revolutionaries. It is traditional, particularly among
people who have not read him, to begin with Gustave Le Bon

(Le Bon 1960). Gustave Le Bon was a French writer who, in 1895, wrote a very short book on the psychology of crowd movements, and this is taken as a point of departure for modern views. But he thinks in terms of a group mind, a concept that would not be very widely accepted these days. and believes that the origins of revolutionary behaviour as such lie in a reversion to primitive behaviour. In revolutions, people are going back to a state of nature, by subordinating their individual will to that of the group, and this group, for Le Bon, actually develops a will of its own. There is very little role for leadership as such in Le Bon but there is very little for politics either, or indeed economics.

A very much more sophisticated interpretation of the relationship of the individual to the group we find in Trotter, who first published his *Instincts of the Herd in Peace and War* in 1916. It is in itself a collection of earlier articles later brought up to date in its 1920 edition by a postscript in which he explains why he thought it was particularly relevant to the conditions of 1920. Trotter is concerned with the reasons why people should act in groups, and he sees these still in nineteenth-century terms, as lying in a herd instinct of gregariousness.

The individual, for Trotter, has three major instincts, or we would now say drives: self-preservation, nutrition, sex. These three drives each tend towards conflict. How, then, can stable human societies exist? Trotter's answer is, there must be a fourth instinct counteracting the other three and compressing the individual into society, and this he calls gregariousness. What is the relationship of the individual member of the flock to its leadership therefore? Trotter says:

'Each member of the flock, tending to follow its neighbour and in turn to be followed, each is in some sense capable of leadership. But no lead will be followed that departs widely from normal behaviour.' [Trotter 1953, p. 16].

Now this of course is acceptable as an explanation as to why people stay in groups and act together, but it does not easily explain why they suddenly depart from normal behaviour and break out of the group. But Trotter has an explanation for that too. There are sub-groups, in other words, within the society as a whole, a herd within the herd; in other words, class. Class, he accepts (as a Marxist would) as being a driving force, in that the individual in subordinating himself to the interests of the class puts that class above the interest of the society as previously constituted. Trotter's book is interesting, firstly, because it has a direct reference to revolution, and embodies an attitude that most popular Western interpretations of revolution have maintained down to the present day. Secondly, it appeared only a year before Freud's *Group Psychology and the Analysis of the Ego* which, after a critique both of Le Bon and McDougall (1920) for lack of explanatory power, gives a view that is theoretically coherent, and hence strikingly different, and has been tremendously influential in very many other ways.

Freud (1965) places a very high, as opposed to a very low, interpretation on leadership as such. He sees it first of all as being a function of the individual. The followers are bound to the leader by the generalised force of libido, a force that can be focused not only on an individual but also outwards, on objects, or things, or organizations, or anything similar. In this case he sees the followers as following the leader because they regard him as their 'ego ideal'. He is what they would like to be. But the leader, on the other hand, Freud sees as having no attachment to anybody. He is narcissistic. He looks at his own reflection and he follows himself, as did the leader of the primal horde. 'He loved no one but himself, or other people only in so far as they served his needs' (Freud 1965, p. 71). The leader is self-motivated, but followers follow the leader as a result of a de-sexualised appeal to primarily sexual motivations. And Freud sees their desire to do this as the desire to substitute the father. It follows, therefore, that the view of Freud is the exact contradiction to the view of Trotter. To Trotter anyone can lead, provided he is doing the right sort of leading and that other people want to follow him, but to Freud only particular narcissistic individuals can do the leading, provided they are attractive to the others, representing to them what they would like to be.

Jung, in his *Psychology of the Unconscious*, first published in 1917, went further (Jung 1933). For Jung, there is a reflection of the idea of the group mind in the form of what he calls 'primordial images' or 'archetypes'. He believes that as a result of many, many generations of living in society, possibly genetically, possibly purely through instruction and fable, people pass on from one generation to another a concept of how they ought to behave, ideas of how things are or, in modern terminology, of roles that people can play. Hence the range of roles or archetypes is limited. There are certain ones that are there, ready for people to play—as for example, the idea of the hero is available for anyone who has the right kind of personality.

Jung's theory of archetypes has proved much more popular, like the rest of his work, with philosophers rather than psychologists. It is valuable, however, because it contributes strongly to the notion of role, which is something that a leader must understand and adopt. There is, moreover, an interesting parallelism between his theory of archetypes and the Weberian concept of traditional authority, just as there is between the Freudian view of leadership and Weber's charisma, and between Weber's notion of legal-rational authority and the interchangeability of leaders envisaged by Trotter.

Secondly, Jung introduced the now familiar terms, 'introvert' and 'extrovert'. Some people are introvert and some people extrovert. Most people are somewhere in between, sharing in each to a greater or lesser extent. Jung sees the extrovert personality as being able to take up through its empirical nature, one of these archetypes and to enact it for the benefit of others; thus, given a reasonable degree of extroversion, a person can act out the part of a leader, and he will attract, therefore, a response from people who are acclimatised to the notion of leadership in one of the particular forms which he is enacting.

The point is that this archetype is also reversed by the introvert. So people will follow the leader because he is doing something that other people expect him to do. William James (1907) put the same thought in terms of a kind of 'tough-mindedness', which is, if you like, a variant of the idea of extroversion—a tough mindedness which enabled one to lead with confidence; to be unaffected too much by considerations of what other people wanted or required but at the same time to draw other people along after one. And in later times of course this translated, by Adorno and his colleagues (1964), into the concept of 'authoritarianism' and the 'authoritarian personality', and related by Eysenck (1963) to political preference.

How far authoritarianism as such qualifies a person to lead is of course a very interesting question, even granted that you accept the concept of authoritarianism. Too much authoritarianism makes a person inflexible, unable to respond to circumstances, and therefore incapable of being followed. So a successful leader would be a person with a fairly high degree, but not an excessive degree, of authoritarianism. To determine which, if any, of these views is correct, we would have to analyse individual revolutionary leaders. But to seek to examine a revolutionary leader clinically would probably lead to a considerable amount of trouble. Also psychologists had assumed that there was something called leadership. Only later did they realise that they were not just looking for leaders but for leaders of *something*. And this varied with the nature not only of the individual, but of the group of which he formed part and the situation confronting it. Secondly, the people who most wanted to know about leadership were military officers, who were looking for military qualities. This limited the general value of the information gained, although it will be of some interest to us because revolution is at least in part a military activity.

In the meantime, people who write on *politics* still tend to think in terms of drives, and instincts, rather than groups and situation. The consensus of the literature is as follows: leaders, on average, excel the group average in intelligence, scholarship, dependability, sociability and/or socio-economic status. The functions of the leader are principally determined by the situation. Problems in the further study of leadership, therefore, basically come down to three possible explanations. no one of which is wholly correct, but each of which depends on the other two. Leadership may be a function of the situation, as Stodgill would have it, or it may, as Gibb has it, be a function of the group (Gibb 1969 citing Stodgill 1948), or it may, as the traditional writers, including Freud, Adler and Jung had it, be a function of the individual. Traditional approaches have concentrated on finding a leadership type. But it does really appear to be a waste of time training leaders as such. It is easier to modify the job they have to do; and that is precisely what the revolutionary leader is in fact doing. The revolutionary leader is not saying: 'here am I, the ideal person to lead the political system as is', he is saying: 'modify the job, and I'll show you which way to go'. So the revolution in fact is about modifying the political structure so that it can be led by people of origins different from those who have previously been leading it.

The second stage is the operationalisation of leadership. In between the leadership as such, or the 'directorate', there are bodies, organisations, groups which can be classified generally as 'staff'. The organisation of a revolution, like the organisation of anything else, depends on its implementation. It is not enough just to stand up on a soapbox at Hyde Park Corner and announce that the revolution is at hand. It is necessary also to create some form of organisation that operationalises the political views that the revolutionary wants to express. In the Leninist view, the reason why revolution succeeds is because the organisation is created. The precise goals can be redefined, can be reorganised at any time, depending on circumstances. What matters is how they are actually put into effect. And this certainly is no less important than the question of which direction the leaders are leading in the first place. There have basically been in the past three different principal approaches to those who participate in revolution. They can be divided, broadly speaking, into: the historical, the psychodynamic and the socio-economic. There are those who explain the fact that a revolution occurred principally in terms of the fact that a specific historical situation generated a response. There are those who attribute the actions of revolutionaries primarily to their own personal circumstances and motivations. And there are those who attribute their driving forces primarily to socio-economic causes.

It is probably not possible to distinguish with a great degree of precision between these categories, because in practice they overlap. We cannot say that any one of them is the principal motivating factor. It is not particularly valuable, certainly, to regard revolutions as 'one-off' historical experiences. This is valid in historical terms, but it is not particularly helpful from the point of view of understanding why people act as they do in the circumstances. One thing is clear, however, and that is that there is a basic difference in scale in all cases from the problem of revolutionary leadership. In the case of revolutionary leadership we are dealing in the first instance principally with small-group behaviour, with how people come to gather small groups around them, to generate forces for the changing of society within these groups, which is how they come to build up organisational bases for revolutionary transformation. When we come to the question of the interaction between the leadership and the mass—a question with which we have already implicitly dealt in our consideration of the crowd and the Freudian view of the relationship of the leader to his followers— we are nevertheless going beyond the limits which experimental psychology will permit us to go. We are going out into a field in which we cannot produce hypotheses capable of being tested by the process of actual experiment. And yet it is quite clear that revolution, in the sense of transforming society, is a question of the organisation of mass action.

From the historical view, there is a great deal that has been written about the actions of revolutionaries in individual revolutionary situations. The problem is relating it to different situations and different historical accounts, and particularly to the most dramatic manifestation of revolutions: the crowd.

The traditional view of the conservative historians was that when crowds became threatening, some kind of demonic possession had taken place: peaceful peasants or happy town dwellers had suddenly been seized by some kind of demon which drove them to revolt against their masters, overthrow the fabric of the state, destroy the structure of society. . . . One finds a much higher degree of sophistication only when one gets down to the study of the crowd in specific historical circumstances. Everett Dean Martin, writing in 1920, was quite explicit about the behaviour of the crowd being only in fact a condition of mind of the individuals, resulting from a mutual consent to do the forbidden thing. In the circumstances of the crowd, where temporarily the crowd decided what was permissible and what was not, people agreed with one another that they would vary the rules of the game and behave differently from what they would have done had they not got the support of the crowd.

This is the reverse of the third theme that can be found even in nineteenth-century studies of the crowd, that is, that the crowd as mass action is to be equated with 'the common people'; that the crowd is an expression of popular will. This runs all the way from the French Revolution of 1789, through our interpretation of the risings of 1830 and the fall of the French monarchy in 1848; and indeed all the revolutions of that surprising year 1848 being characterised by crowd action, the one common assumption that all historians seemed to take for granted was that these crowds were somehow made up of 'the common people', whoever they may be. It is therefore very interesting to find in Rudé's studies (1964) that his view of the crowd in the French Revolution and in England in Luddism and Chartism, and anywhere else where he has studied it, is that on the whole the crowd is a group of sober citizens, including craftsmen, journeymen and apprentices. And in fact it is representative of the more solid classes; it is skewed towards representation of the more well-to-do, as a political party is, but it is not of course in any sense a direct carbon copy of the total population.

Furthermore Rudé, through his historical investigations, has been able to demonstrate that the crowd in fact not only was not a mob of the hairy unwashed who had suddenly risen in revolt against the structure of decent orderly society (which was always implicit in all previous studies of crowd action, particularly those written by academics), but was simply not consistent from one incident to another. The crowd differs. In, say, the situation of the Reveillon Riots, where people were rioting about the price of bread, there was a predominance of wage-earners because this was what affected them most closely. In the march on Versailles it was the market women and in the attack on the Tuileries, the action which actually brought down the structure of the French monarchy, the people who dominated the crowd were the workshop masters and the apprentices—in other words, this was an industrial action, very definitely resulting from the galloping inflation created by the issue of paper currency (*assignats*) and the general incompetence of the French government at managing its economy. So that although in each case crowd action and riots take place, they are really both forms of political action, each of which involves crowd participation, but the crowds in each case are different.

The Gordon Riots of 1780, which did not bring down the British government, originated in peaceful political organization, at least by eighteenth-century standards. The crowd was formed from the mass rallies of a body called the Protestant Association, which the fanatic Lord George Gordon, the younger son of a ducal family, was organising in resistance to the rumours which were then current that Catholics might perhaps be allowed to vote or perhaps have some representation in the state. He opposed this and, since he was a good orator, whipped up enormous numbers of people into a frenzy of hostility. This mass hysteria culminated in one of his huge rallies which descended on the Houses of Parliament and, among other things, pulled the Archbishop of York out of his coach. (Only the fact that he was grabbed by well-wishers and passed from hand to hand over the top of the crowd saved him from being mauled.) One or two of the peers were rather badly hurt in the process, and the crowd in the end, now frustrated, turned on Newgate Prison, broke it open, released a lot of prisoners, and burned down a distillery. Eventually the whole thing broke up when they started drinking the spirits that poured out of the burning distillery, and people fell about, blind drunk in the street, and were easily dispersed by government troops (Hibbert 1958).

Here we can draw a sharp distinction between the crowd as such—that is, all the people who happened to be present in front of the Houses of Parliament on that day in 1780— and the effective crowd, the people who happened to be engaged in political action. Because of course the whole point about a crowd is that it is a very substantial body; it is very difficult for crowds of any size to achieve anything very complicated. Thirdly, one of the extremely interesting things about the French Revolutionary crowds is that, quite apart from their class composition, they were unusual in other respects. Firstly, the members were unusually old by the standards of the time; the average age of the crowds at the siege of the Bastille was thirty-four, as near as can be ascertained, on the basis of those who joined up in the Paris Sections, where close records were taken. Obviously we cannot rely on those too closely; there must have been a lot of people who got into the records who were probably not there on the day and indeed may not have even been in Paris on the day. But Paris in 1789 was still a relatively small city. People must have known fairly well who was there and who was not, and must have had to produce witnesses, so this is as good a study of the composition of the revolutionary crowd as we are ever likely to get. And thirty-four certainly was old in 1789. The crowd at the Bastille were not the skinheads of the late eighteenth century, cutting loose. Its age composition indicates a degree of maturity in political thought which is extremely interesting. And these, by the standards of the population of the day, would have been the maturer and more responsible members of society.

The second point is that we know, because people had to sign the book when they signed up in the Paris Sections, that a very substantial number of them could write. In fact, measured by their ability to sign their names, rather than make a mark in the book, literacy runs in some of these incidents as high as 80 per cent. Now it can be argued that some of the illiterate ones may in fact not have turned up. Well, that may be true, but it is very interesting to note what a very large number of people—for the late eighteenth century, when mass education was by no means one of the features of pre-Revolutionary society in France—were able to read and write. So the *sans culottes*, in other words, were not, by our standards, the working class. They were indeed very much the bourgeoisie, seemingly confirming the Marxist view that the French Revolution was a bourgeois revolution, and a forerunner of the modern followers of populist leaders such as Perón's *descamisados*, or Vargas' *o povo* in Brazil.

Now the problem with extrapolating from this study of the crowd is that the circumstances of the French Revolution are undoubtedly unusual. The fact that we know what happened when crowds were gathered together in the French

Revolution does not mean that we know everything about recruitment in revolutionary conditions. We still do not know exactly how all these people gathered together, how much their action was an impulse, or how much the product of long-term circumstances. We do know that on many later occasions attempts to reenact the French Revolution in other circumstances did not come off. For example, on at least one occasion, the French government survived because a timely shower of rain dispersed the rioters. That was in 1830. Interestingly enough it happened again in 1961. The crowd is unreliable from the revolutionary point of view, and the fact that it is effective in certain circumstances should not be taken as indicating that it is by any means the sole vehicle through which revolutions come to express themselves; as we will see later, they are only really part of the action in the condition we call urban insurrection.

Given the size of the crowds, given their haphazard nature, given on the whole their political responsibility, which must lead them in general to want to maintain the existing system with only small amendments, and given the fact that too many hands simply cannot move the levers of the state in anything but the crudest sense of the word, we have to assume that, when it comes to collective action, anomic groupings of any kind lose out to formal organisations. Therefore, most later revolutions have been organised and led, or captured and taken over and directed, by formal organisations. The structure of recruitment into formal organisations is a very different matter from that of crowds.

As noted above, historical instances show that far and away the most common element that participates in political revolutions, is the professional armed forces—the most disciplined, best-organised and most well-trained sector of the population. They seem to be followed at rather a far remove by civilian institutional groups, that is, groups of civilians, frequently working with the military, sometimes working independently, who have a common interest by virtue of their occupation or work. Least important and least significant are the civilian associational groups, whether the political parties or organisations like Lord George Gordon's

Protestant Association. The pressure group is the weakest element and the weakest source of revolutionaries.

This then leads us on to the question of the sociological factors determining recruitment. Dahrendorf talks of latent interest groups in society, and regards these, in terms which I think would be very widely accepted, as being fodder for mass action where the shared exigencies of the group appear salient (Dahrendorf 1961). The problem with this is, determining, firstly, what shared exigencies are, and secondly, at what point they become salient. Once more, in examining revolutionary action it is very difficult to determine whether it is revolutionary or not until a revolution has actually happened.

The notions shared of exigencies and their saliency is of course a general formulation from a number of different sociologists' views. We can put first into this category the deprivation of economic resources, as cited by Marxists. In other words, if revolutions are created by mass action in the Marxist sense, they are created by the fact that the proletariat is being increasingly deprived of the means by which it lives; the proletariat which is itself defined as being that section of the population which has no economic resource except its children (*proles*) and its work. Increasing deprivation, therefore, leads to the desire for revolt, the circumstances in which revolt is possible, but there is still no effective revolt until the point at which it is given direction and 'made aware' of its state of deprivation.

Durkheim, deriving many of his ideas from another aspect of Marxist thinking, in particular Marx's theory of alienation, appears to regard the impulse for revolutions as arising from deprivation of identity (anomie). People in modern societies, unable to regard themselves as individuals by the nature of their society, therefore, turn to mass action as a means of redressing this deprivation (Durkheim 1965). This view has been developed further by the elite theorists.

In Mosca and Pareto one can see the shared exigencies as being the deprivation of access to power (Meisel 1965). If the individual cannot attain political power he will turn to mass action as a vehicle for his demands.

For the individual, in each of these three cases, the common factor is deprivation of educational advantage. It is the one thing on which everyone appears to be agreed. The most serious deprivation is illiteracy, or, secondarily, functional illiteracy (i.e. one has enough education to be able to write one's name or read a newspaper headline, but is effectively unable to make use of the cultural mechanisms of one's society). The next most serious is an inadequate basis for assessment of one's own circumstances. It is education that allows the individual to handle the mechanisms of social control by making up his own mind about things and forming his own views. If the mechanisms for social control were wholly effective, a functionalist would argue, clearly revolution in any broad sense of the word must be impossible, because people are unable to form a view that is contrary to the generally held views of their society, and it is impossible therefore for them to wish to revolt against it.

The question is, what do we find then is the role of education in revolutionary conditions? Clearly it is no accident that the principal theorist of the French Revolution—the man who is always quoted, who was always regarded as a virtual substitute for divine inspiration—namely Rousseau, was not only the author of *The Social Contract* but also the author of *Émile*. The philosophical basis for the development of revolutionary ambitions lies in an awareness of the inadequacy of society to provide the mechanisms by which people can obtain access to economic resources, identity, or power, as the case may be. Whichever we consider, the vehicle remains education.

How far then is it necessary—for revolution to take place —for this educational process to have reached? Smelser regards the revolutionary event proper, the kind of chain of circumstances that formed the French Revolution or the Russian Revolution, as being primarily concerned with the reorientation of the fundamental norms of society. It is not sufficient, even for a revolution to occur, for anything less than these to be changed. Indeed, revolutions are about even more than that, about changing the fundamental values of society, about altering the entire intellectual basis (Smelser 1962). I do not think we can necessarily go quite as far as that, in that there have been revolutions that have developed initially from rather more limited objectives, but have gone on to lead people to question the assumptions on which their society was based. This can be seen, for example, in the period from 1830 to 1848 in France. In 1830, the July Revolution, there is a simple change of monarchy and a belief that political changes in themselves are going to be sufficient. In 1848, although the political changes are dramatic enough, the abolition of the monarchy and the introduction of a Republic is seen as a further step in the social development of the country. The Revolution is accompanied by the setting-up of workshops and the assumption that the state has now taken on the responsibility for looking after the interests of the unemployed. This is a new sphere of influence and the basis of all subsequent ideas of the role of the state in social welfare.

The change of values, as such, however, does not necessarily lead people to political action. In certain circumstances, and perhaps in most, it leads participants directly to mass action but not necessarily governmental action. A common form of the desire to change the values and norms of society is, for example, the religious revivalist movement, which is not necessarily revolutionary and may indeed be counter-revolutionary. For action to become revolutionary in the political sense of the word it must first involve the further step of the identification of exigencies with the policies of the government of the day. It is not sufficient to feel that the values of society have to be changed, it is necessary for people to have determined that it is the government itself that is maintaining those values through the establishment of norms that implicitly demand the maintenance of values to which they no longer adhere.

The extent of the impact of this decision depends on the extent to which it is felt possible to change the government. And this, of course, is a much more difficult question. The true importance of Marx in these circumstances lies probably less in his belief that revolution is a vehicle of social change (because many people always have believed that), but in the belief in its certainty to result in historically inevitable and hence favourable social change. And it is this belief in its certainty that is at one and the same time Marxism's greatest

strength and its greatest weakness. The historical examples of
the degree and direction of social change which are possible
in revolution, now that we have more historical examples
than were available to Marx at the beginning of 1848, are
distinctly discouraging. The degree to which society is fundamentally transformed in any state is much less impressive
than it might have seemed then.

If violent change is routinised in a state, as it is indeed in
many Latin American states and in the Middle Eastern states,
one may well have a degree of political change. But an
awareness of the possibility of frequent government changes
in fact militates against the association of political change
with social change. Similarly, it could be argued that it is
precisely the instability of French governments in the past
that has limited the degree of social change that has occurred
in France.

Deprivation (Gurr 1970) is related to expectation. The
Davies J-Curve is a simple attempt to model this in purely
economic terms (Davies 1962). But the problem is that
in revolutions we do not know what people's expectations
are, we cannot ask them beforehand: 'What did you expect?'
In the circumstances in which some people are attracted to a
revolutionary movement, what matters is not just how many
are so attracted, but how many people are attracted to any
other possible solution, and especially, how many people
are attracted to the policies being pursued by the state
(cf. Gamson 1975). The social causes of revolution do not
relate primarily to who is to be recruited into the revolutionary movement. They also relate to who is to be alienated
from the government. In what sense, therefore, do people feel
the government is failing to fulfil their needs? And how small
a carrot do they need from the government, in fact, to
become totally apathetic? Because if the majority of the
nation is apathetic then a relatively small governmental group
may battle it out and the result can go either way.

The problem is, then, one of the opposition creating a
winning coalition. How easy is this, and in how many ways
can it be done? Marx saw this winning coalition as resulting
from the fusion of the ideas of the intellectuals—the direction, the sharpness and the organisation, which they could

lend to the movement of the proletariat—with the mass power of the proletariat itself, the people who produced goods, who did the work. They were the fundamental element of the coalition, but they could not be effective without direction. There has been comparatively little work done on the possibilities of other coalitions; there is a great attraction in numbers and the proletariat looks, on the face of it, like the most revolutionary class. Yet it was Engels himself who pointed out that in fact the bourgeoisie was the most revolutionary class in the circumstances of his day (Marx and Engels 1962). It was from its ranks that the men who were actually overthrowing governments came, engaged in the process of reshaping society so as, he argued, to liberate the productive forces implicit in the bourgeoisie itself.

Yet it was not until Hitler in this century constructed his own lower middle-class/military coalition that it became so obvious that this particular aspect had been overlooked. The idea of the massed power of the workers had blinded people to the fact that other alternative coalitions within society can provide sufficient foundation for the seizure of political power. And in fact in contemporary Brazil, as in contemporary Argentina, there is a very deliberate attempt to reshape society on the basis of a very different sort of coalition, overriding the interests of the workers in the interests of a nationalist goal. Such a middle-class alliance with the military in fact owes many of its roots to the same kind of forces which in the past, in other circumstances, created, for example, left-wing movements in Germany in 1919–20 and in the Russian Revolution.

All governments are the product of a successful coalition. The success of the elite assures that of its coalition. It does not have to carry out a revolution because it is already in power. We deduce that this is the kind of political alliance that has the most chance of success.

Lastly, then, let us turn to the individual motivation of the recruits. Why do people follow revolutionary leaders? Leaders certainly may be maladjusted, they may be narcissistic, they may be crazy, but surely all their followers cannot be?

Firstly, we may accept that all organised society implies

a degree of what Putney and Putney (1964) have called 'normal neurosis': if you live in a normal society you have to be neurotic. You have no alternative if you are going to adjust to a society which demands that you compromise at every turn on what you would like to do. Then, there are, as I began by pointing out, three views as to the relationship of leaders to followers, and to the situation. Out of these we can derive three psychological mechanisms by which the leader in fact relates to his followers, and the followers to the leader.

In the Freudian scheme, the follower identifies with the leader, he takes the leader as his 'ego ideal'. He would like to be the leader; he regards him therefore as a cathectic object and he identifies with him, as being something that he would like to be but cannot be.

The second mechanism is the mechanism of projection. The follower is having psychological difficulties—to be human he must have psychological difficulties—he therefore projects his psychological difficulties onto figures who represent authority. He acts out his complexes and uses the mechanism of projection to externalise them onto the outside world. And because he projects his difficulties onto figures representing authority, he develops a degree of opposition to those figures, and so he follows a leader who will oppose those figures.

And thirdly, there is the concept of authoritarianism. Authoritarianism is generally seen as being a statement about leadership. If you say 'So-and-so is authoritarian', you are usually referring to him as a leader figure. He sends you rude memos, does not wait for a reply, is ready to blame you, is impervious to argument, and so on. But the point about authoritarianism as a concept is that it has a great deal to say about people who are not leading. It is more significant, if anything, as a statement of why people accept authority, rather than why people take up authority and undertake authority. It is a statement about why people submit to authority; authoritarianism in the follower leads him unquestioningly to accept what the leader does, leads him to wish to submit to decisive statements about what is to be done, thus enabling him to avoid having to take psychological initiatives to determine his own place in the world. As Michels (1959) argued, the mass want the burden of leadership removed from them, and are collectively grateful.

Now these three statements are all statements about how people realistically act in real situations. But another aspect that has become very much part of the modern psychological armoury is the fact that people substitute practical action —that is, realistic action in a realistic assessment of the circumstances—with dramatic action—that is, in circumstances in which one either cannot see or prefers not to see a path of action that is realistic.

People act out roles, and therefore if Robin Hood is there to be followed, men can accept the part of one of the Merrie Men who follow him. Cowboys require Indians. One accepts the most appropriate role within one's ideal of what society is about. One takes part in the play because the play helps pass the time; the play can be used as a substitute for the more uncomfortable problems of reality, or because it is generally more fun.

So people can, therefore, look at leadership in more ways than the mechanism of identification would suggest. They can accept leadership because the leader represents for them what they would like to do but cannot do. They cannot run the hundred yards in world record time. They are not liable to win a gold medal at the Olympic Games. They are not likely to become Prime Minister. They are not likely to land on the Moon. Identification is one possible response, but there are others.

The second is the most obvious one, that the leader is doing what they would very much like to do; and not just what they would like to do but cannot. It is something that they want for themselves, but are happy to have him or her get, if they cannot. If they cannot be Prime Minister and they know they cannot, then they accept that he should be Prime Minister rather than anyone else. Eva Perón's rich furs and jewels represented this sort of vicarious satisfaction.

And the third kind of leader, who is also a common type in revolutionary situations and therefore one has to think about the implications of people following him, is the leader who acts out what people ought to do but are not really trying to do. The religious leader, like the Ayatollah Khomeini, is typical of this. People do not really want to be good, moral or uplifting, but it salves their conscience considerably to have other people going around being good, moral and uplifting. They do not really want to attain the standards of sainthood, but they are very happy to have a saint around the place, whom they can feel they are trying to live up to without actually having to go through the strain of doing it.

No one of these three situations perhaps satisfactorily applies in full to any real person. Each of them has some relevant aspects. But one further contribution which seems to me to be of particular interest in the revolutionary situation is the question of why any of these psychological mechanisms should particularly relate to revolution as opposed to anything else. In other words, why do people suddenly develop the urge to go out and fight, when they are shown the way?

The fact is that revolution is essentially a product of the lack of alternatives. If you can change your government then you do not vent your feelings on that government, you simply change it. If you can change your society—you suddenly get the idea of sweeping away whatever is restraining you, and you *can* do it—then of course that cause for aggression disappears.

Finally there is the international dimension. A great many people are atracted to revolutionary causes in the case of the great revolutions but what really makes them difficult is the presence of an external threat. In other words, we find the mass mobilisation of hostility to an aggressor who represents all that people regard as being worst in their society *but*, being outside their society, there are no taboos preventing them from venting their rage on them. The French aristocrats, for example, were hated, not just because they were *aristos*, but because they were seen as Austrian sympathisers. The French projected their hostility to the Austrians onto a domestic object, and blithely cut off the aristocrats' heads since they must be foreign spies. There was then no limitation to the extent to which their aggression could take practical form, and the same held true in the Russian case when external intervention also occurred.

The experience of foreign travel seems, historically, to have been important in forming the political perspectives of revolutionary leaders. It acted to liberate them from the constraints and assumptions of their own society, and left them ready to take up the international current of ideas, which included revolutionary ideals and example. The way in which such ideas were diffused to the mass of potential followers is, however, a much more difficult question to assess. In open societies, such cultural diffusion is normal, and can, as in pre-Revolutionary France, prepare the way for very radical shifts of ideological perspective. In Austria or in Russia at the same period, the same ideas were indeed known, but confined to a very small section of the ruling elite. They were not widely available to the mass of the population, and the state took good care to ensure that they were not. The introduction of French Revolutionary ideas into Germany and Italy, therefore, was not attended by the same major changes that took place in France, although a generation later they were to produce their own intellectual climate of change which had a very different, nationalist coloration. Application of these findings to current circumstances should suggest to the student of international relations that the widely-held view that revolutions can be propagated unchanged across national boundaries is not only likely to be wrong, but is almost certainly the exact converse of the truth; and that the only thing that could make it possible would be the nationalistic response generated by the attempt by an external power to suppress revolutionary feeling by invasion or attack.

6 Three forms of revolutionary action

At this point I propose to discuss in further detail the three main forms of revolutionary action as the student of international politics is actually likely to encounter them. This will incorporate at the same time a critique of the principal views generally held about each. In turn I shall consider the coup, guerrilla warfare, and urban insurrection.

THE COUP

The coup is something so alien to British politics that there is no English word for it, and it is often wrongly confused with a related concept, that of *coup d'état*. But *coup d'état* means, in the strict sense, a seizure of a disproportionate share of the state power in a sudden stroke of force by the existing government; for example, Louis Napoleon's seizure of power on 2 December 1851, which is practically the type example. He was already President of the French Republic and he made use of military forces at his disposal to proclaim himself Emperor and then held a plebiscite afterwards to 'legitimise' the action. In practice the word *coup* (which means simply 'blow') in French is used in many other phrases, *coup de main*—blow of the hand—meaning a rapid military stroke, a seizure of a point of advantage without warning; and there are many others.

In English, when we talk about the sudden seizure of power by anyone, we can therefore loosely call it a 'coup', but it is not a very precise definition. There are many more types than appear on the surface and there are different sorts of coup. The Latin Americans, some of whom go in for coups, distinguish between three main types of activity (Stokes 1959).

First of all they distinguish *Cuartelazo*, which is the seizure of power by barracks revolt. *Cuartelazo* means literally 'a blow from the barracks'—'*azo*' being a Spanish ending which means a blow (*martelazo* means the blow of a hammer, for example). Secondly, there is the *golpe* which is the Spanish for coup, properly speaking. The Spanish *golpe* is simply a quick seizure of state power by a small group, which may or may not be military, but usually is. But there is another important, not quite so precisely definable, term, *pronunciamiento*, where a section of the provincial military pronounces against the central government. This is Spanish rather than Latin American in origin for *pronunciamentos* were very common in nineteenth-century Spain. They mean that the military pronounce against central government and then wait and see how much support they can get from other provincial military circles to cause the deposition of central government.

These are all different forms of action, and there are probably many others. We have to consider what the coup is and there is general agreement that it is in form essentially a tactical military operation. In the case of Luttwak's *Coup d'Etat* (1968), as we have already seen, the coup is treated almost entirely as a tactical military operation. Luttwak's general thesis is, it will be recalled, that the coup is, in fact, the use of a sector of the state machine to seize control of the rest—generally speaking, the use of a portion of the military to displace the existing government.

The corollary of this thesis is that the governmental machine depends on its continuity; therefore the action of a coup in political terms is to remove the incumbent government, and put another government in its place so quickly that no-one has time to complain about it. This is not altogether true, and in some respects it is not true at all, but it is the general thinking behind the idea of the coup and it is the kind of way in which coups sometimes do operate.

The second corollary is that the coup as such is politically neutral; that the politics of the government are irrelevant; that, in fact, the coup can only take place in states where there is insufficient attachment to the ideological bases of government for it to matter very much which sort of government is actually in power. Therefore, one government can be removed and another government put in its place without any serious dissension that cannot be suppressed by the military or police.

What Luttwak is talking about, then, is a quick seizure of state power, using one sector of the state machine; secondly, something that is ideologically neutral. It is therefore represented in his book (which is frivolous in tone) as being something that any fool can carry out with a bit of fore-thought and planning, and in fact his book is subtitled 'a practical handbook'. A joke is a joke, but some of Luttwak's other implications have to be studied much more carefully.

Firstly, Luttwak's assumption is that, as a tactical military operation the coup is basically about the use of military force; therefore, he says, the distinctive feature of it is that one must do it quickly; therefore one must commit all one's forces, and cannot afford to maintain a strategic reserve. This may be true, but Luttwak derives from this the assumption that there is no need for any kind of headquarters organisa-tion, separate from the actual force carrying out the coup. Now this, as we saw in Chapter 1, in military and strategic terms, is unsound. But in any case, it is fairly evident that it is not, in fact, what coup leaders normally do. Most coup leaders are military officers, generally of high standing within their respective military forces, and they usually assume command of the operation from headquarters, such as they might use for any other military operation. In fact it may not be stretching the point too far to say that these are often almost the only important military operations that the military carry out, in the countries in which coups are prevalent.

The fact is that the military coup cannot be detached from a consideration of the very special nature of the military organisation itself. In the first place, the military are an arm of government; indeed in earlier times in all states, and again in the new states, they are overwhelmingly the most import-ant branch of government. They combine exceptional resources born of the need or desire to defend the state with the symbolic importance they therefore can claim as custo-dians of national independence, unity and purpose. Because their business is national security, they have the right to keep all that they do secret, which includes their ability to conspire against the authorities, be they civil or military.

Secondly, military forces have a very distinctive form of organisation, centred on a special group, the officer corps, who are trained and recruited separately in order to ensure the automatic and unquestioning obedience of those they command. Educated together in special establishments from their early adolescence, the officers have a strong sense of *esprit de corps* and are overwhelmingly influenced by the concept of their membership of the armed forces as an organisation. Indeed, such is the *esprit de corps* of each service, that inter-service rivalry, where the army, for geostrategic reasons, has to admit the existence of other services to the political process, is one of the few factors acting to restrain military intervention or prolonged military control of politics. For the military officer the service is much more important than any other formative influence, so much so, in fact, that some Third World Marxists have actually wondered if the armed forces do not constitute a separate class, with interests and motivation of its own.

Thirdly, therefore, participation in military politics becomes a necessity for the individual officer in a politicised army, such that his entire personal career, on the one hand, and the future of the social order, on the other, both come to be regarded by him as subordinated to the needs of the military institution. This in turn becomes an institution that is very highly bureaucratised (cf. Feit 1973), in which the highly structured nature of the military society makes the conduct of the military coup increasingly formalised. It therefore ceases to be a military action for military motives, and becomes instead by degrees a highly stylised demonstration of military power designed at one and the same time to remove an unpopular government from power with the minimum of fuss and military casualties, and at the same time to make it clear to the civilians that they must not and will not be allowed to intervene on their own account— hence the soldiers at street corners, guards on public buildings and rounding-up of student and trade-union leaders that characteristically accompany a military coup.

The next problem of the coup is that of preparation. Pre-planning is of the essence. It has to allow for three things: first of all, the handling of a continuous flow of information;

secondly, the implementation of contingency planning. And thirdly and most importantly, the exercise of political, as opposed to military, control over the population, because a coup that simply succeeded in displacing a section of the government without in fact actually being able to establish political control would obviously, in political terms, be ineffective, though partially or wholly successful in the military sense. Again coups are frequently complicated, in political terms, by several types of military action going on at the same time.

Now, what are the principal operational problems of the coup? The first is timing. Luttwak wants no headquarters organisation because he seems to think that is superfluous, and hence potentially dangerous. Yet he requires a strategy which is flexible in order to 'take advantage' of the situation. In particular, he sees (accurately) the need to assimilate accretions of strength in the event of success, or risk the possibility that they will then form a loose element in the political situation which may accrue to a rival and bring about a counter-coup. The seizure of power must be followed up by the effective 'neutralisation' of all other centres of power, otherwise the first action is likely to initiate a coup-sequence in which various people scramble for power and the end product may not be what the coup promoters had originally intended.

The second thing is that Luttwak sees a military conspiracy as a series of 'go/no-go' decisions; a coup has to be planned with a series of cut-off points, at which, if the circumstances are not favourable, the leaders will be able to cut it off. And yet, if the leaders are actually in action and no separate headquarters is maintained, it is difficult to see how they will be able to stop the coup, once initiated. And it seems likely that Luttwak (although in theory incorrect here) is, in fact, putting his finger on a very serious weakness of military coups, and that is, that like other military actions, they are very hard to stop once started. In other words, once the die is cast and the troops are actually in action, there is no getting out of it—for one thing, the act of initiating a military coup is treason and to commit treason means, of course, reprisals. So the leaders are, in fact, committed to the extent that the whole essence of the coup depends on the success of their forward planning; either they were right in their series of assumptions or else they are in trouble and the last 'go/no-go' decision is really the decision to launch the coup.

Luttwak obviously does not find this very satisfactory, so he then proposes that instead of operating as a single group, the coup promoters should operate as a series of teams.

Our teams will emerge from their bases and proceed to seize their designated targets while operating as independent units; their collective purposes and their coordinations will thus remain unknown until it is too late for any effective opposition. The leaders of the *coup* will be scattered among the various teams, each joining the team whose ultimate target requires his presence. [Luttwak 1968, p. 139.]

In other words, the forces will operate in teams but the leaders will themselves be leading separate teams, each in a separate place. For example, one has to go to the presidential palace in order to raise the national flag; another one has to go to the local radio station in order to make the approved broadcast announcing that the military have taken over, and so on. This is evidently what does happen in practice. But it presents certain problems, as in the case of the attempted military coup in Mexico in 1913, in which one of the two leaders of the coup *was* marching confidently towards the presidential palace under the impression that the defenders of the palace were going to surrender to him and that their shots were purely token resistance, when one of them shot him down and killed him. So incidents of this kind can happen and some things that go wrong in military coups, which are, after all, at least potentially fatal, can also result in destroying their whole political point.

Luttwak emphasises that each of these teams should, in his view, operate separately, carrying its own equipment with it, should be planned to operate as an independent entity, and that the co-ordination should allow for 'lead time'. For example, the presidential palace must have been captured before the leader turns up to announce that he has taken over power, otherwise things might get difficult. And in practice, one frequently finds that military coups fail for just this reason. Far more military coups fail than succeed.

Luttwak's targets are given a classification as (A), (B) and (C). (A) targets are 'heavily guarded facilities with strict pass control'—like the national palace, army headquarters, the central police station. They are, in other words, essential zones of control for any effective incumbent government, but they are also necessarily the most heavily-armed portions of the government apparatus, and therefore they cannot necessarily be taken by direct frontal assault. Indeed, it is extremely improbable, given the fact that most military installations are designed, after all, for defence in international war, that they can be successfully stormed using local forces. Therefore we see that one of the prime reasons why the military are, in fact, almost exclusive promoters of successful coups is quite simply that they have day-long access to these facilities. In order to gain access to these heavily-armed targets, they have to be infiltrated, but they have to be infiltrated by members of the military and therefore essentially this is a military preoccupation.

The (B) targets are communications targets. In Luttwak's view they can be neutralised by technicians operating in small teams making use of sabotage. Luttwak's whole theme is— you cannot safely hope to suborn the military unless you are a member of the military (and not always then). If, therefore, you wish to become a coup promoter (something he seems to think is highly desirable) then you have to concentrate on what you can get hold of, which is communications. These play a key role in the history of the development of the coup.

In the seizure of power in Russia in 1917, Trotsky made extensive use of the ability to cut the incumbent Kerensky government off from peripheral military installations by simply cutting off the telephone and other services. And after the coup the promised Constitutional Convention was put out of action altogether because a technician turned off the lights and went home and they were all left sitting in the dark! Now these experiences gave rise to a doctrine which Trotsky (1966) propagated later—that the real centre of power, the real key to the control of the modern state was its communications. He thought particularly in terms of telephone and telegraph. But first of all one must remember that 1917 came before the invention of broadcasting; radio was still used primarily for military communications purposes, and it was very imperfect. Secondly, the pieces of this doctrine were first picked up not by Trotsky and his followers, or indeed by communists in general, but by Mussolini. The famous Mussolini 'March on Rome' depended on the development of this technique which was not only the control of communications, but the saturation of communications, by a blanket of misleading messages to the effect that the Fascists were marching on Rome and were going to take over. This so scared the incumbent government that they collapsed without much resistance, and the King called upon Mussolini to form a government when he arrived peacefully in Rome by sleeping car!

It was Curzio Malaparte, an Italian newspaperman who had in fact seen this Mussolini technique in action at first hand, who wrote in 1927 a book on coups (Malaparte 1932) which was then widely popular and which is now, alas, out of print, in which he too stated that the key issue was the control of communications. To avoid the problem of actually fighting the government, one simply blew up the communications network and the government would collapse. Malaparte was partly right in that communications are obviously important, but he was also seriously wrong. It is possible to put the communications network out of action to a considerable extent but, as explained in Chapter 1, most governments do in fact have a considerable back-up facility, and more so in modern times. Secondly, the monopoly of communications that might have been possible in 1917 is no longer practicable, certainly in any developed country. When Luttwak suggests that a coup could take place in *any* country, this has to be taken in context. It could not take place in this way in any highly-developed Western European state or in the United States, because there are too many levels at which the state machine operates, and too many back-up facilities. Moreover, communications work both ways, so it is not just a question of putting communications out of action for the incumbent government, but maintaining them for the revolutionaries. In 1918 Lenin, for example, was able to use the telephone as Kerensky had not, to rally the troops to the defence of his government.

And the last point, again noted above, is that the symbolic importance of targets was not fully recognised by Malaparte as it was by Trotsky. It was not sufficient for the October Revolution simply to cut the Kerensky government off; it was necessary for the Winter Palace to be captured in order to demonstrate to the people of Petrograd that power had in fact been seized. In Mexico in 1915, Venustiano Carranza was able effectively to control something like nine-tenths of the national territory, in so far as anyone could control the national territory of Mexico at that particular time, but he could not maintain a viable government in Mexico City itself. Hence, until he had actually succeeded in capturing the national capital, he was not able to convince outside observers and a large section of the population that he was, in fact, effectively in control. This is even more true of the smaller countries than it is of large ones like Mexico.

The third category of targets that Luttwak mentions is individuals to be detained for the duration of the coup. These he envisages as being put out of action, 'picked off' by small teams operating ahead of the main forces. In other words, the scenario for a Luttwak coup goes something like this: all of a sudden people leap out of corners, seize individuals and detain them; then columns start converging on strategic targets, putting them out of action one after the other. Meanwhile, technicians are busy blowing up communications centres. Finally, there is a kind of set-piece in which the main centres are captured. This appears to be a fairly large, co-ordinated military organisation, no matter how you look at it, and it is certainly hard to reconcile with the advice Luttwak gives at the beginning to the coup promoter that he ought to ensure that word of these intentions does not leak out beforehand.

Then there is the question of where the troops come from. Luttwak's principal consideration here is the possibility of treachery before the event. He remains sanguine: he says, suborn the technicians (he obviously does not have a very high opinion of technicians) but steer clear of the regular military. What you are going to do when the regular military are needed to go out and form all these teams and columns, of course, is not stated.

He then proceeds to say that the real risk is at the moment of action, and one can see why. Because if the leaders of the coup are all disposed in their various columns, then it is going to be very difficult for them to keep a check on what is going on. So, therefore, both during and after the coup, he recommends that coup promoters should keep their troops busy. It is the traditional public-school remedy for all ills: keep the troops on the move, give them plenty of organised activities and they will not be able to get up to mischief. And so a set of secondary targets should be provided so that the moment they capture the primary target they have to hare off somewhere else to capture the secondary target; and this stops them from getting together and mutinying.

The second key to the control of troops during the action and immediately afterwards is to monopolise their hold on communications, and ensure that all communications with individual columns come directly from the leaders. But, as already pointed out, the leaders are actually *in* the columns, so how can the leaders maintain vertical communications without maintaining horizontal communications with one another?

And lastly, on the purely military aspects, there is the question of the arena. Luttwak suggests that the limits— the perimeter of the arena—should be defined by road blocks or other means, so that the military activities going on inside cannot be hampered by inconvenient problems like the arrival of reinforcements from the neighbouring town. He conceives his entire strategy in terms of the governmental defence of this perimeter, which the coup forces have to penetrate rapidly and without warning.

Now this does not, in fact, happen. Where, in the past, the military have got into the habit of making military coups, there is more often than not a barracks very close to the centre of the capital city with a good route direct to the centre of government, for example, Campo de Mayo in Buenos Aires. What therefore tends to happen in a coup situation is that the troops are already in the capital. They are so near to the centre that they do not have to worry about things like road blocks and there is no question of forces actually coming in from outside. In the case of the *cuartelazo*, the 'blow from the barracks', this is the barracks that the blow comes from.

We must now consider the political issues. The principal political problems of the coup revolve around the thesis of destabilisation versus restabilisation. There are already two basic and opposing theses; the first one, which I shall call the 'Malaparte thesis' is the idea that there is a technical separation of government from their command structure and that the seizure of power mainly involves the neutralisation of communications, and so the neutralisation of the government. The emphasis is therefore on the (B) targets and their neutralisation. The second is Luttwak's thesis itself which emphasises the heavy (A) targets which are of both physical and symbolic importance, and communications are treated as a secondary prerequisite to the acquisition of the arena, in which the main battle for the control of the (A) targets will be fought out.

Neither of these two writers seem to think a great deal of the (C) targets, but in fact it is the (C) targets that are the key to the whole exercise, since the rapid removal of the president of the republic and his exportation to the nearest point of the globe where he is likely to be welcome is, in fact, the most common form of all military coups. There are numerous examples, of course, of these. I should like to mention only one famous one that went wrong, which was the case of Alberto Lleras Camargo, the President of Colombia, who was seized by a small force of military rebels, flung into the back of a jeep, and driven off rapidly towards the airport to be put on a plane. As it happened, on their way out, they went past the front of the presidential palace and were stopped for speeding by a traffic policeman who looked in the back, found the President of the Republic there, called up reinforcements and freed him. So the coup failed.

The (C) targets therefore, it seems to me, are the key to the political success of the coup, which is basically about removing the officials of the existing government. I stress 'removal'; political assassinations are not distinct in their effects from coups but coups do not normally mean the assassination of prominent leaders of governments. Many people think that coups are normally extremely blood-thirsty, whereas, in practice, deaths during coups are usually accidental or, one might say 'incidental' to the main purpose. It is very seldom government leaders who get killed in coup-prone countries, and exceptions like the overthrow of the King of Iraq (1958), the fall of Allende in Chile (1973) or the bloodshed that always seems to accompany coups in Syria, are in fact conspicuous precisely because they are exceptions. This is not, in fact, the usual way in which things happen.

After the coup, the next question is 'how is political power acquired?' Well, firstly, the source of power comes from the removal of the existing source of power. Then political allegiances necessarily have to re-form around the existing situation. If the incumbent government is no longer there, then it cannot command allegiance in the way that an effective functioning government can. Coups frequently fail if incumbent governments jump fast enough to get out of the way and then simply call upon their established political support to rally to them. Even the most unstable government in Latin America prolongs its life for anything up to six months or a year by jumping out from under the first military coup that comes along, and it survives often until the sixth, seventh or eighth.

Secondly, Luttwak throughout regards the source of power of a coup as coming from the state itself: 'A coup consists of the infiltration of a small but critical segment of the state apparatus, which is then used to displace the government from its control of the remainder.' (Luttwak 1968, p. 24.)

Now this may be in part true if one regards the state apparatus as a unity, but the idea of an apparatus is probably unhelpful. The whole impression is rather mechanical. There is a mechanical analogy, if you like, but the mechanical analogy is rather like a Judo throw; the way in which a coup occurs is by making use of the inertia of the machine to bring it down.

Lastly, then, Luttwak produces three preconditions for a successful coup. Firstly, that 'the social and economic conditions of the target country must be such as to confine political participation to a small fraction of the population'. Political participation must, in other words, be limited. This is realistic, because a coup most usually does not occur in countries with broad political participation. Where coups have occurred in such countries, they have generally occurred (as in 1940 in France) in cases of grave national emergency, when, in other words, participation was momentarily suspended. The military coup—or rather, the coup in a situation in which the state as a whole is paralysed for some external reason or other—is a quite conceivable idea. This seems a realistic assessment; political participation must be limited if coups are to be successful. The broader the political participation, the less likely the coup; but even a country like Uruguay, where political participation had been broad for many years, sustained a violent deformation in its government in 1973 (though this deformation was not in the nature of a military coup in the sense in which, for example, the fall of Allende in Chile was a military coup). The operation of the broad participation itself varies the terms in which the seizure of political power is possible. It has to take place in a different kind of way and with a much greater degree of mass participation, which by definition is not a coup, though the events in Uruguay have been termed, appropriately in some ways, a 'soft coup'.

The second point is very interesting because there is one very good modern example which points the lesson and that is the case of Gabon. 'The target state must be substantially independent and the influence of foreign powers in its internal political life must be relatively limited', writes Luttwak. In 1963, the government of Gabon was overthrown by a military coup. President Mba, however, was able to get word through to the French; the French rushed in an expeditionary force and set Mba back on the presidential chair of Gabon. Here is a clear example of the reversal of a coup by direct external intervention—a much more direct and interesting example, incidentally, than the American intervention in the Dominican Republic in 1965. But the French, for some reason, never get blamed for their intervention in Gabon, whereas the Americans never cease being blamed for their intervention in the Dominican Republic—which suggests something very interesting about international politics!

Luttwak further writes that: 'The target state must have a political centre. If there are several centres these must be identifiable and they must be politically, rather than ethnically, structured.' In other words, military coups in Nigeria are likely to go wrong. And the evidence of what has happened when there was a military coup in Nigeria shows that this was probably substantially correct. All kinds of things went wrong; the coup failed to impose a new regime, although the Head of State, General Ironsi, was killed, and the dislocation of the state was such that it was one of the major contingent factors in the rise to the secession of Biafra, 1966–7.

Lastly, 'If the state is controlled by a non-politically organised unit, the coup can only be carried out with its consent or neutrality.' In other words, if it is a military government, the military have to support the coup or be neutral, and the same can be presumed by extension for a secret police organisation. So, in other words, the existence of a powerful repressive secret police would suggest that coups can only be carried out in a country with the connivance or tacit consent of its secret police.

Quite apart from the many technical questions impeding replacement of governments and these restrictive preconditions which are political conditions, it is also an important question as to whether there is in fact a very wide range of governments that would automatically be obeyed by the state machine. Luttwak says: 'The apparatus of the state is therefore to some extent a machine which will normally behave in a perfectly predictable and automatic manner. A coup operates by taking advantage of this machine-like behaviour during the coup because it uses parts of the state apparatus to seize the controlling levers and afterwards because the value of the levers depends on the fact that the state is a machine.' Common sense, however, suggests that it cannot be assumed that, for example, in a normally strongly right-wing country a very strongly left-wing government would necessarily be obeyed, or vice versa. It is true to say that the value of the levers on a railway engine depends on their being attached to the rest of the engine, but equally, they depend on having steam in the boiler, and a track under the wheels, and a whole host of other things. In other words, you cannot use this analogy without being struck by its enormous limitations.

It would clearly be extremely awkward if no one realised that a coup had in fact happened, and went on as before. Coup promoters therefore necessarily make use of the media to issue a statement of goals. Usually they accompany this by proclaiming a period of curfew which results in complete immobility; forcing upon people a reappraisal of their predicament in circumstances in which they are exposed only to official statements, generally interspersed by patriotic music.

Luttwak distinguishes four types of manifesto and these four types do indeed seem to correspond to some political reality: the 'romantic lyrical', the 'messianic', the 'rational administrator' and the 'unprepared'. They all have the common theme of governmental corruption, degradation of national life, the prevalence of vice and immorality.

To sum up, therefore, there are three aspects of restabilisa-tion. It is first of all necessary to stop the revolutionary forces in their takeover of power, or else the coup promoters would be in trouble. It is, secondly, necessary to get the state bureaucracy functioning again and to get the state operating like a state. And lastly, it will be necessary to get the public back to work, a problem which is not confined, of course, to the events of the military coup.

GUERRILLA WARFARE

There are of course all kinds of ancestries claimed for guerrilla warfare. One of the favourite and most fashionable nowadays is fifth-century China, but there are, in fact, others. The point is that it is difficult to distinguish guerrilla warfare from ordinary warfare until very recent times, and the reason is quite simple, that the development in regular warfare from about 1780 onwards, by the introduction of heavy artillery, has changed the nature of ordinary war; it has not in the same respect changed the nature of guerrilla warfare. And guerrilla or partisan warfare was often a feature of earlier wars, if the circumstances rendered it possible.

The major change has been the disappearance of the siege, the last major example of siege warfare being perhaps the First World War with its static lines. With the disappearance of the siege, regular forces revert to mobile combat and the guerrilla has an opportunity to attack them. Here I propose to begin with that aspect of guerrilla warfare that particularly reflects the development of the European tradition. For it is in Europe that the term originated, in Spain to be precise, in the Spanish War of Independence which broke out on 2 May 1808. It followed the successful invasion of Spain and Portugal, the capture of the Spanish Monarchy by the French and the imposition of Napoleon's brother as ruler of Spain; and it was a war of independence in the same sense that the Serbian War of Independence or the Egyptian war against the Turks or any of these other early nineteenth-century nationalist wars were.

The Spanish War of Independence, however, notably depended on two kinds of fighting. The Spanish component, which had largely been pre-empted by the success of the French invasion and the capture of the regular seat of power in Spain, consisted of the organisation of irregular forces. These were, in turn, sustained by Spain's allies in the field— a certain number of regular forces under Arthur Wellesley, later First Duke of Wellington, starting out from Portugal and eventually driving forward into Spain, supported by the 'little war' or 'guerrilla' of the native Spanish irregulars.

The guerrillas gave rise to a Spanish mystique. They were the Spanish component; they were the element that actually represented the Spanish contribution to the War of Independence. As Raymond Carr says in his history of Spain, the war 'gave liberalism its programme and its technique of revolution. It defines Spanish patriotism and endows it with an enduring myth. It saddled liberalism with the problems of generals in politics and the mystique of the guerrilla.' (Carr 1966, p. 105.) Their success was therefore directly related to a political party within Spain, that is, the *liberales* or the liberals, as they became more familiarly known later. Their appeal was nationalistic in flavour in that it called upon the resources of the support latent in the Spanish countryside for a fighting force that would drive the French out; the French as foreigners were clearly identified as such, and guerrilla warfare was directed against them. Thirdly, the guerrilla 'little war', was conducted by small groups of forces.

One very important point about the Spanish uprising was that it did secure a very early symbolic victory, which is often important in a long drawn-out content. The first Spanish victory occurred in July 1808, at Baylén, and it was a product not just of Spanish prowess but of French incompetence. It was Napoleon's belief that the conquest of Spain was, to use Carr's words again, 'a police operation that could be entrusted to inferior troops' (ibid., p. 106). Napoleon had in fact sent one of his most loyal but least able marshals to Spain. The bulk of his forces was at that time on the Austrian and Russian fronts. However, the immediate response of the French to the defeat was to send better troops, and with good troops they won repeatedly. The pressure that this put on the allied effort was extremely interesting. Time and time again Wellington believed that he was being betrayed by the Spanish and his irregulars, whereas time and time again the Spaniards believed that the English were merely pillaging the country and doing very little towards its liberation. In other words there was, from the beginning, a dichotomy between the irregular forces of the Spanish and the regular forces of the allies.

Yet the liberation of Spain required both: the guerrilla was essential to the defeat of the French. 'It was this continuous resistance, feeble as it often was, which broke Napoleon's doctrine of maximum concentration in the attempt to solve contradictory demands of operation and occupation in the hostile countryside.' (Carr 1966, p. 108.) Spain would have been powerless without Wellington's field forces; Wellington could not have operated with such a small army without the diversionary effects of Spanish resistance. It was the Spaniards who proved Wellington's own maxim, 'the more ground the French hold the weaker they will be at any point.' With allowances, this could almost have been written by Mao Tse Tung. In other words, the guerrilla element in the Spanish War of Independence converts enemy strength into weakness. It wore down the French and it destroyed what should have been their greatest strategic advantage, their concentration. By concentrating forces, the French finally found they had increased their dependence on their supply lines rather than decreased them. As they increased their dependence on their lines of supply so the lines of supply themselves became more critical and were correspondingly more vulnerable to Spanish operations.

The Spanish guerrilla war was in fact one of the largest recorded in terms of the size of the forces. The Spaniards deployed up to, perhaps, 50,000 men altogether, organised in bands of up to 8,000—a very substantial guerrilla force indeed. But even then it proved very difficult to use them other than tactically. They were a raw force and because of the very poor communications, the use of guerrillas in co-ordinated military activities proved almost impossible. They did, therefore, operate primarily as independent units. Even then the French were able to hold them at a certain level because the French enjoyed means of communication superior to any other nation in Europe at that time. They had interior lines of communication and they made use of the semaphore. From semaphore towers on every hill they could signal with moveable apparatus from one hill to another, which of course was very much quicker than the guerrillas could signal to one another by runner or on horseback. So that superior communications were the secret of the long French resistance rather than the concentration of military forces that went with it.

But the guerrillas also had one very important additional effect. Their function was to reoccupy areas evacuated by the French and to impose a 'patriot terror', bullying the population into resistance. Each time the French moved out of an area the guerrillas would move in, fill the vacuum and punish any French collaborators, thus ensuring less collaboration next time the French came by. In other words, the possibility of being vulnerable to a terrorist movement once the French had gone away, was something that severely restricted collaboration with the invading forces.

I have gone into some detail about this case for three reasons: firstly, because the instance is unfamiliar; secondly, because it explains the origins of the word; and thirdly, because it has a very definite, direct relationship with three of the major modern areas of insurgency. Of these, all are former Spanish territories and the communication links between them and Spain are quite manifest. In fact, they are so manifest that we have to be rather cautious, because it may not be that the idea of guerrilla warfare was actually transmitted from Spain to its colonies. It may merely have been that the social conditions in the colonies were similar and that most of them copied the same kind of methods. In the former Spanish territories one identifies three areas in particular.

Firstly, there are the Latin American countries which generally became independent in the nineteenth century. Here, in fact, the legacy of guerrilla warfare goes on throughout the nineteenth century. It is responsible to a considerable extent for the ultimate defeat in 1825 of the Spaniards in Peru itself, where Spaniards enjoyed a considerable degree of support; but their support was gradually eroded by irregular forces operating over a very wide area. Later it brings the liberals to power in many countries, as in Guatemala in 1870. And in resistance to foreign attack, it is very successful in wearing down the French occupation in Mexico in 1864–7. These are three examples of the use of guerrilla warfare tactics, which confirm the value of the method in Latin America itself in the nineteenth century. Another legacy of the Spanish War of Independence in general politics, a product of war with very small forces, was that of the Caudillo, the military leader of the nineteenth century. It is one of the major disadvantages of guerrilla warfare that it tends to place military leaders or militarised leaders in politics.

Cuba was the one state in Latin America that did not get independence with the rest. In fact it was known as *La Isla Siempre Leal* or 'The Ever Loyal Island'. But in 1868, at the time of the collapse of the Spanish monarchy and the imposition of the republic in Spain itself, the rather conservative Cubans got impatient. They decided it was now time for them to fight for their independence and they were helped in this by sympathisers in the United States. From 1868–78 there followed the Ten Years War—a war of independence which in fact did not succeed. For Cuba did not have an indigenous Indian population. It did have a large, mainly Afro-American population built up out of imported slaves. Thirdly, slavery was still legal in Cuba at this period and was therefore a powerful reason for other countries to begin to support the War of Independence in Cuba for purely idealistic reasons; but it was not yet sufficient to bring success.

In 1895 the War of Independence was resumed as the result of a small expeditionary movement led by the famous patriot José Martí. Martí, whose poetry is still read today, was not only an inspiration to the movement of Cuban independence, he was also its first real leader (Martí 1968). His career is remarkably similar to the career of all kinds of other guerrillas and can serve as a type example.

First of all, he was gaoled at 17 years of age for laughing at some Spanish soldiers. This sort of incident is quite familiar. One only has to think of Andrew Jackson, later President of the United States, who at the age of 14 was ordered to black the boots of a British officer during the American War of Independence, and when he refused to do so, was hit across the face with the officer's sword, leaving him scarred for life. He later turned out to be the American hero of the Battle of New Orleans (1815).

Martí was not hit across the face with a sword, but he was put in gaol. After he got out he fled, left Cuba and built a Cuban revolutionary party among exiles in the United States, which he financed by going on speaking tours. In February 1895 he landed in Cuba with his pocket Cicero and a couple of revolvers. Sadly, he soon fell into the hands of the Spanish authorities and was put to death; but his separatist movement survived. In his last letter to the people of Cuba he expressed his main fears; firstly that, the danger of Cuba lay in that, when it attained independence, it would fall under the dominance of a military leader, a military Caudillo, like the other Latin American countries; and secondly, that in any case it was too near the United States not to be subjected to its power, like David to Goliath. (That seems a curious metaphor to use but it was in fact what he wrote.) Martí's inspiration stirred again in the two experienced military leaders who had both fought in the Ten Years War. Gómez and Maceo recruited from the rural areas groups of black and poor white forces, the classes which had traditionally taken to the hills when there was no economic future for them. And they received through filibustering, arms sent in small ships from the United States, which the Spanish fleet could not intercept.

The Spanish forces faced, among other things, lack of any roads—since they had foolishly not built any—jungle war, rain, and disease. They sent there instead (as always on these occasions) a General, General Weyler, to *pacify* the Cubans by military means. Weyler set about pacifying them vigorously, with all the guns he had available. To prevent them receiving supplies he herded the civilian population into *campos de reconcentración*, concentration camps. (It should be noted that, when originally invented, 'concentration camp' meant a place where the civilian population was concentrated: ever since 1944 the words 'concentration camp' have come to mean 'extermination camp'. They are two very different things, and it was Weyler who used concentration camps for the very first time, not—as may be found in some textbooks —the British in South Africa.) Weyler was subject to abuse from all sides, not only from Spain, but from outside and he is quoted as saying rather bitterly 'How do they want me to wage war? With Bishops' pastorals and presents of sweets and money?' (Carr 1966, p. 385).

With Martí killed in battle, the whole picture could have been black indeed for the Cubans if it had not been for two fortunate events. Firstly, Canovas, the Prime Minister of Spain, was assassinated by an Italian anarchist in 1897. When his government fell apart, the liberals were converted to the principle of autonomy but were unable to form a working coalition to continue the war. Finally, the United States picked a quarrel with them over the explosion of the USS *Maine* in Havana in 1898. The Spanish–American War broke out, and the Spanish were resoundingly defeated. Cuba was freed, but immediately became an American protectorate.

The third area affected by the Spanish experience is that of the Philippines in south-east Asia which, between 1898 and 1902, waged a guerrilla war against the Americans. The reason was that the Americans had bestowed their forces in readiness for the Spanish–American War in such a way that they had forces in all major Spanish strongholds and an obvious one was in Manila Bay in the Philippines. This was the only south-east Asian colony of Spain and it was also an important naval base. If the Americans pulled their ships out of the Pacific to send them to the Atlantic to fight against Cuba instead, then they would risk having to fight a two-ocean war. What they did was to direct Admiral Dewey, who happened to be in the region, to attack Manila Bay and capture it, and surprised the Spanish so that resistance collapsed very quickly. The capture of Manila Bay therefore left the United States Government in nominal control of the Philippines, but the Philippines, of course, now wanted to become independent too. They in turn therefore had to be pacified and *were* duly pacified—it took four years to end guerrilla resistance but it was done. And so the Philippines remained an American possession down to 1946 when they became independent. In the years between 1945 and 1948, however, a further guerrilla movement arose which, though to a considerable extent pre-empted by the American decision to give the Philippines independence in 1946, necessitated the commitment of American forces, available as a result of the end of the war in the Pacific.

Thus, the Philippines in the post-war period forms one of the four major areas of insurgency in south-east Asia; the other three being the Indonesian War of Independence, 1945–8 (Nasution 1965), the August Revolution in Vietnam, 1945–54 (Giap 1965) and the Malayan Emergency, 1948–60. There are distinct resemblances between all these movements, and so great was the similarity in fact, that at the time they were generally put down to communist machinations. Certainly there were communist moves to encourage revolt and there were substantial communist elements in all these movements. But there was also, though not greatly appreciated at the time, a great reservoir of feeling for independence. The western powers had been humiliated in the Pacific; they had been soundly defeated by the Japanese and humiliated in Singapore. The loss of prestige which this meant was in itself sufficient to result in independence, for example, for Burma.

The development of guerrilla warfare seems to have come easily for the British, probably because they did not maintain a large standing army as such. Where they did maintain a large standing army, in India, there was the greatest possible resistance to any irregular warfare. In the Second World War Wingate and his Chindits operated quite naturally on the further side of the Indian Empire, purely on native wit and their experience of the First World War, but they were always greatly distrusted by the establishment in India itself. Yet in doing so they drew on this native tradition, and the role of one man in particular, T. E. Lawrence (1926). It has been suggested that it is with Lawrence, as far as the Western tradition is concerned, that guerrilla warfare actually developed from being just a convenient technique into a doctrine about how to wage war by every possible means.

Lawrence's theory about guerrilla warfare is interesting because he emphasises two points. Firstly, that the main purpose of guerrilla forces, unlike conventional forces, is not to engage the enemy. They must be capable of protecting themselves against the enemy and they must harass the enemy, but they must not engage the enemy. There is no thought here, therefore, of using guerrillas as partisan forces in the sense in which, for example, Clausewitz would have permitted their use; nor in the sense which Mao uses forces, in that they will actually be developed into a conventional army. Rather, he is thinking along the lines of a political process that will make it politically inexpedient for the Turks to remain in possession of the Arabian states. Secondly, to attack the enemy is to destroy their supplies and lines of communication; to destroy their machinery is to destroy their importance and to destroy them. Lawrence's small forces, drifting around 'like a gas', were particularly at home in the Arabian territory as they could easily disappear into the civilian population. If guerrillas are to do this they must have a civilian population to disappear into. In South Vietnam, when everyone of fighting age was called up for military service, the only people actually left, who could sink into the background, were women and children—hence the very widespread use of children on the insurgent side in South Vietnam. Boys who are not yet old enough to be called up are still able to shoot people, but they have to be trained first. Also, in Arabia in Lawrence's time, space was a tremendous advantage; there were no aircraft as yet, and his forces could hide in the desert where no one could pursue them, since they did not have the transport.

Although Lawrence was very much a side-show in the First World War and we cannot really talk of guerrilla tactics being used in the War anywhere other than Tanzania, they did turn out to be terribly important even so. For one thing, the tragic, heroic nature of Lawrence's career made him a very attractive character, he knew a lot of the right people, and he wrote well, so that the next generation in Britain grew up feeling that Lawrence had been badly treated, as well as the Arabs. And secondly, the Second World War was not a static war like the First. In mobile war, states collapsed very quickly, leaving a great deal of their social structure intact. They changed hands very rapidly and it was possible to keep guerrilla forces in being on the edge of the main theatres of conflict to perform an important role in holding down regular troops. And the Chindits, who at first proved unpopular with the British regular military establishment, afterwards turned out to be very much more valuable than people realised, and in fact they helped protect the flank of India itself.

But guerrilla tactics had an added disadvantage, and this was not fully realised until after 1945. It made, not only politically active, but also militarily active, a great many local inhabitants who, after the war, had been conveniently issued with British guns and military equipment generally, carefully trained in military techniques, who, in addition, had had four years' free experience in fighting the Japanese. They were then able to enforce their own political opinions, which they proceeded to do, rifle in hand. The result was the Malayan Emergency. The MPAJA, as it originally was, the Malayan People's Anti-Japanese Army, was simply transformed into the Malayan Races Liberation Army (MRLA), aimed at the British instead of the Japanese. It took out the same guns as it had before, disappeared into the jungle, and set to work. And again the technique was very similar to Lawrence's, to blow up the roads and railway lines. To keep the railway lines clear, cars were run up and down the lines fifteen minutes in front of every train. At first the guerrillas blew up the armoured cars; later they let the armoured car go by and there was a good chance that when it had gone through the train would be there, so they could attack the train itself. In 1950 the High Commissioner, Sir Henry Gurney, was ambushed successfully, though quite unintentionally, since it appears from the captured documents and the information that is now available that they *thought* they were shooting up the military commander (Short 1974).

This is of course a tendency that guerrillas must resist— shooting up important people just because they happen to be there! One can say that Sir Henry Gurney's death in fact saved a great number of lives, as far as the British forces in Malaya were concerned, since it forced them to get organised in a way that they had not done before. And the same kind of thing happens repeatedly in other circumstances where guerrillas—for example, in the case of Guevara's expedition in Bolivia—make the mistake of hitting an important target too soon and actually alert the government to the urgency and the necessity of doing something about them. Circum- stances often deteriorate such that guerrilla movements are ultimately defeated. Far more have been defeated than have been successful.

The same period saw the emergence, with Mao Tse-tung, of a new kind of guerrilla warfare as a political technique. Mao profited from indigenous Chinese experience and his extensive knowledge of Chinese history and of the Chinese past. Secondly, the heroes whom he followed (and he did follow heroes) were specifically Chinese heroes who had fought against foreigners. Thirdly, Mao's technique of guerrilla warfare was tested, as it were, and given its baptism of fire, in combat with the Japanese. The Sino–Japanese War of 1937–45 is the real beginning of the Second World War. For Europeans it began in 1939, for the Americans and the USSR in 1941, but for the Chinese it began in 1937, and some Chinese regard it as having begun in 1932, when the Japanese originally invaded Manchuria. And the alliance of nationalist partisan forces through the countryside was not only the natural, but the obvious thing to do. They were fighting an interntional war against the Japanese: it was a war of national liberation.

The theory behind it, developed in Mao's book *Guerrilla Warfare*, appeared in 1937 (Schram 1963). It is here that he develops his famous three-stage model of guerrilla organisation. It begins, firstly, with organisation, consolidation, preservation of base areas, and creation of a network of sympathisers by the training of volunteers and the agitation and propaganda in the surrounding countryside. The second stage envisages the progessive military expansion of the base areas, making use of sabotage, liquidation of 'collaborationists' and 'reactionary elements', and the seizure of medical supplies and equipment from forces, from outlying police posts and weak columns. The expansion of the base areas, then, is effected by sabotage, liquidation of 'collaborationists' and 'reactionary elements' and the seizure of arms, ammunition and supplies. And this is in fact very close to Lawrence's view. You can see the convergence here between the two practical doctrines, each worked out in actual combat. The expansion of the peripheral liberated area, however, was quite unLawrentian, as Lawrence did not believe in the liberation of areas at all, as being quite contrary to his notion of effective guerrilla warfare. The question is, was Mao right or was Lawrence right? For Mao, the expansion of the liberated areas takes place by a useful technique of expanding the militia faster than the regular army. It is the militia that sabotages the immediate surrounding countryside, liquidating collaborationists as it goes. Because there is a regular military effort behind it, it expands rapidly through the countryside in what is termed the 'oil-spot technique'.

The climax is the destruction of the enemy by the transformation of guerrilla forces into an orthodox military force capable of defeating the government in pitched battles. And this will be supplemented by the protraction of the phase of development into conventional forces and the re-training of the military under cover of negotiations. Now this is very relevant in connection with the enormous hysteria that was raised in the West after 1968 about the terrible Americans who could not possibly take seriously the desire of the Vietnamese for peace. The Vietnamese, happy peace-loving people that they were, were no doubt sincere in their desire to negotiate, even if in doing so they negotiated away some of their own positions, but they also proceeded to reorganise the guerrilla forces in South Vietnam into conventional forces so they could hold strategic lines, under cover of the negotiations technique. When that failed, in 1972, they called in the North Vietnamese army.

Mao emphasised that the use of negotiations would be for purely military purposes. This is indeed the purpose of using negotiations, not to reach a fair and just decision, whatever that may be—unless the term 'just decision' means to expand regular military forces, and wear down the opponent's morale.

Mao's work is based on three basic preconceptions: firstly, the doctrine of strength and weakness to which I have already alluded. You turn your weaknesses into strength and the enemy's strength into his weaknesses. This is done by a number of means, but primarily by surprise. The expression is 'Uproar in the East, strike in the West'. In other words, you send men around to make a loud noise on one side and you attack on the other side—that is a technique older than Mao, and probably older even than organised government in China. The second preconception (the most dubious one) is that guerrillas will have full information and that the government will have no information; that the guerrillas will succeed in denying all information about themselves to the government while, through their own network of sympathisers, laying open the strategic and tactical state of the government to themselves.

Now, as an ideal this is excellent, and under conditions of international warfare this is probably very nearly possible. But times have changed since 1937—aircraft were already in those days reaching a sufficient level of sophistication to be used as spotters. Now the major powers have earth satellites, infra-red detectors, guided missiles, thinking bombs and napalm. Psychological warfare has been developed, and many governments have not stopped short of using torture. The chance of a guerrilla being able to deny all knowledge of his activities to the government is now in fact very much less than it was in Mao's time. So anyone following his advice will be in trouble, unless they remember the last point that Mao makes, that guerrilla warfare is not mainly to defeat the enemy—it is to mobilise the people and to turn them into a revolutionary force. This is the great difference between Mao and anyone else, except perhaps Lawrence, who as far as that goes regarded the Arab role in the fight against the Turks as being an essential part of creating an Arab nationalism which was not already there.

There is little practical detail in Mao. There are, however, the Three Rules and the Eight Remarks. The rules are that 'all actions are subject to command', 'do not steal from the people', 'be neither selfish nor unjust'; they are general precepts. The Eight Remarks are specific ones:

Close the door when you leave the house;
Roll up the bedding in which you have slept;
Be courteous;
Be honest in your transactions;
Return what you borrow;
Replace what you break;
Do not bathe in the presence of women;
Do not without authority search those you arrest.

It is only undisciplined troops who make the people their enemies [says Mao] and who like the fish out of its native element, cannot live. [This is his famous fish-in-water saying—usually put the other way round.]

For practical information on guerrilla warfare, therefore, we must return to Cuba, the Cuba of Fidel Castro and Che Guevara. Che Guevara, an Argentine by birth, had studied medicine before travelling via Bolivia and Guatemala into exile in Mexico, where he met the Cubans planning their return to their homeland. In actual combat he became a military leader himself, directing the crucial 'Battle of Santa Clara' which in late 1958 proved the decisive psychological stroke in the campaign against President Batista, and shortly after victory he wrote his account of the campaign (Guevara 1968b) and a short handbook for the guerrilla fighter (Guevara 1967). Both stress the very practical approach he brought to the subject, but the latter also enunciated three principles which were to be of much greater theoretical appeal. They were:

1. Popular forces can win a war against the army.
2. It is not necessary to wait until all conditions for making revolution exist; the insurrection can create them.
3. In underdeveloped America the countryside is the basic area for armed fighting. [Guevara 1967, p. 2.]

This was a heady message for his admirers. It was not necessary, they believed, to create a party or even a trained army, and Guevara himself rejected the idea that his followers should come from one social class. All that was needed was a small group of guerrillas. This was the theory of the *foco* (focus), a small group as the vehicle of social revolution, elevated to a doctrine by a French-born Professor of the University of Havana, Régis Debray (Debray 1965). It was to exercise a profound influence on insurgents in Latin America and the rest of the Third World well into the 1970s, but as Guevara's own death in Bolivia showed, it was dangerously wrong.

Why then was it so popular? Some of the reasons were of course cultural: it was a call to battle that could hardly be rejected without seeming faint-hearted. But much of it was its seeming practicality. So much of what Guevara wrote was very practical indeed:

A small notebook and pen or pencil for taking notes and for letters to the outside or communication with other guerrilla bands ought always to be a part of the guerrilla fighter's equipment [he wrote]. Pieces of string or rope should be kept available; these have many uses. Also needles, thread, and buttons for clothing. The guerrilla fighter who carries this equipment will have a solid house on his back, rather heavy but furnished to assure a comfortable life during the hardships of the campaign. [Guevara 1967, p. 55.]

As Luis Mercier Vega wrote, the book is 'rather a strange mixture of traditional precepts, an elementary exposé of the principles of military training for NCOs and recruits, nostalgic descriptions of life in the open air among men, and the kind of enthusiasm engendered by ex-servicemen looking back.

In particular, there is a sort of exaltation of sweat, steaming feet, and suchlike, which would bring back memories for any 1914–18 veteran or infantryman with experience of something besides asceptic [sic] war' (Mercier Vega 1969, p. 76).

The seeming practicality overlaid the invalidity of the theory. It was true that in Cuba the guerrillas had come before the party, but then not very many people before 1959 had realised that they were fighting for a party, since at this stage not even Castro himself could be described as a Marxist–Leninist, despite his later comments on the subject. More seriously, however, the Cuban Revolution was not in fact a victory for guerrilla warfare, for its contribution in practical terms was minimal. What eventually defeated Batista was the mass withdrawal of support by the workers in the cities and the inability of the regime to control, not peasants, for there were very few of those in Cuba, but the organised plantation workers, that had no real parallel even elsewhere in Latin America.

When it came to the test, however, in the Bolivian campaign, it is hard to say whether the trial of guerrilla warfare failed because of deficiencies in the theory or practice, as the evidence of different accounts (Guevara 1968a, González and Sánchez Salazar 1969, Harris 1970) agrees that almost every mistake that could have been made was made.

On the strategic level, the decision to pick Bolivia, on a false analogy with the Sierra Maestra, took no account of the rigours of the climate and the mountains. There were peasants in Bolivia, certainly, but they had benefited from the Revolution in 1952 and had no wish to risk their gains. Besides, they were suspicious of white-skinned bearded Cubans (or Argentines), who reminded them too strongly of the *Conquistadores* who had taken their lands in the first place. Even if they had been successful, Bolivia offered too weak a base from which to advance on the rest of Latin America, as they plainly hoped, and they had no support from the urban workers.

On the tactical level, errors were legion. They had learnt Quechua, at least, so that they could talk to the Bolivians in their own language, but they picked as site for operations Ñancuahuazu, where the peasants spoke Guaraní. They attacked a government force before they themselves were ready to defend themselves. They took endless photographs of themselves, which, with much of their other supplies and the vital evidence that linked them to Cuba, fell into the hands of government forces. Even the most trivial mistakes proved fatal; for example, 'Tania la guerrillera', apparently both a KGB and an East German agent in her spare time, was killed because she wore a white shirt in the middle of the green jungle and presented a perfect target to her pursuers. And Debray's own visit confirmed the importance of the group to the Bolivian authorities, but not before it had shown up the weaknesses of the group's position: 'The Frenchman', Guevara himself wrote, 'was somewhat too eloquent when he described how useful he could be to us outside' (Guevara 1968a, p. 132). Che himself clearly tried to keep up morale as long as possible, ignoring the uncomfortable realities. Thus he wrote on 30 April that a dog, 'Lolo died a victim of Urbano's temper: he threw a rifle at its head'. In his analysis of the month of May he wrote that 'The dogs have shown themselves to be incompetent and have withdrawn to civilization' (ibid., pp. 151, 164).

The failure of the rural guerrilla dream was to lead to a brief attempt to transpose its principles to the urban setting— to create, in short, a new form of insurgency called 'urban guerrilla' warfare (Oppenheimer 1970). As the sudden death of its chief figure, Carlos Marighela showed, its theory, sketchy as it was (Marighela 1971), was even less securely founded. Urban terrorism could be a considerable nuisance to a government, but at no time did it threaten its survival, and it did create a powerful reaction in favour of repression. It is not, however, to be confused with urban insurrection, which has quite a different history and rationale.

URBAN INSURRECTION

Urban insurrection is clearly distinguished from the other two forms of warfare. Firstly, unlike guerrilla warfare, it occurs principally in cities, and secondly, unlike a military coup, it involves armed mass uprisings, and this is its basic distinguishing feature. The existence of urban insurrectionary movements of more or less spontaneous character is associated particularly with the so-called great revolutions, and in particular, with the French and Russian Revolutions. Features which are related to the question of armed mass uprising are these:

1. First of all, the existence of a condition of dual power; that is to say, the creation by mass action of competitive political organs, or the enlargement of existing organs, into a political structure (competitive with the existing regime). Examples are the Paris Sections, the Russian Soviets, and trade union movements generally, in conditions in which they have been associated with revolutionary mass action.
2. Secondly, there is the phenomenon of the general strike, first employed in Italy in 1907. There have been numerous examples of countries in which general strikes have occurred since, and one theorist, Sorel, held that the general strike itself was the truly proletarian way to overthrow a government and to bring about political change (Sorel 1950).

   However, general strikes in this particular context tend to be associated with mass action, or to be a form of mass action which is particularly associated with the involvement of the proletariat and therefore of particular interest if one is studying revolutions from a Marxist ideological base.
3. Lastly, the third of the three associated features is convention leadership, that is to say, leadership of the movement by a large body in which alternative policies are publicly canvassed, be it a party organisation, a central committee organisation, or a body such as the National Assembly or the National Convention in France.

There are precursors of modern urban insurrection in the numerous urban movements of early modern times—for example, the Fronde in France—but if one wants to study the history of urban insurrection one must draw a sharp line in 1789, and say that the definitive example for all modern purposes has tended to be the French Revolution of 1789. The Revolution itself was a product of the shifting coalition of political forces which was continually acting in opposition to mass unrest, and mass unrest periodically erupted into political action and impinged upon any attempt to try and create a stable political system. So that, in fact, the most democratic of the French revolutionary Constitutions, the revolutionary Constitution of 1791, was never put into practice, because it could not survive in opposition to the actual physical power of the Sections which led eventually to the setting up of the Committee of Public Safety.

There are six incidents in particular between 1789 and 1792; two, first of all, in 1789: the storming of the Bastille on 14 July, and on 5 October, the march on Versailles when the royal family was brought back to Paris by the crowd. Then in 1792 there is an important series of four incidents of mass action. First of all came the unsuccessful attack on the Tuileries on 20 June which was repulsed, the King covering himself with great distinction. On 11 July mass action broke up the Paris Council and destroyed the municipal government of Paris, thus laying open the way for the lack of central control which led to the storming of the Tuileries on 10 August. That, in turn, virtually meant the end of the monarchy; and lastly, between 2 and 7 September, followed the so-called 'September Massacres' in which a great many people perished who were not aristocrats or royalty and really had nothing to do with political action at all—it was the occasion of the paying-off of old scores. The September Massacres led directly to the creation by the National Assembly of the Committee of Public Safety.

Once the Committee of Public Safety had come into existence it is significant that the future course of the revolution no longer involved mass action on a successful level. The next major uprisings against the French revolutionary government, the Bread Riots of 1 April 1795 (the Twelfth of Germinal), were suppressed. So were the riots of 20 May (the First of Prarial), and finally on the famous Day of the Sections, which was 5 October 1795, the crowd was dispersed with the celebrated 'whiff of grapeshot' by a young artillery lieutenant called Napoleon.

People had, however, already learnt from the French Revolution the lesson of the effectiveness, as they thought, of mass action. It was believed that mass insurrection on a sufficient scale was, in fact, the distinguishing feature of those revolutions that were successful. In 1830, Charles X was overthrown by a mass rising of Parisians who seized the *Hotel de Ville* and raised the barricades on 29 July. Thiers, the parliamentary leader who had led the protest against Charles X's dictatorial acts, was completely outflanked: the parliamentary protest was not the immediate cause for the fall of Charles X. Similarly, between 22 and 24 February 1848, a spontaneous revolt sufficed to topple Louis Philippe. And the lesson was, therefore, reinforced for most Frenchmen and a great many European observers that revolutionary action meant mass urban action. The mass rising of urban dwellers against their government was in itself what constituted true revolution.

Two other incidents offered different lessons. First of all, between 23 and 26 June—the 'June Days' of 1848—a further rising occurred against the Provisional Government. But the National Assembly gave dictatorial powers to General Cavaignac who suppressed the revolt with considerable brutality. The 'June Days' therefore ended in massacre.

Secondly, it so happened that the leader of the parliamentary revolt in 1830, Thiers, was the man who became head of the Provisional Government of France on the fall of the Second Empire in 1870. And it was he who was the first modern statesman to understand the roots of the problem for previous governments confronted with revolutionary mass action of how to understand and how to counteract it. When Thiers was confronted with the appearance of the Commune on 18 March 1871, he already had troops in Paris, where they repeated the example of previous detachments, except for the fresh troops led by Napoleon and Cavaignac, and began to fraternise with the spontaneous revolt which they encountered. The fraternisation was in itself sufficient to stop Thiers from successfully suppressing the Commune on 18 March. Thiers, however, responded to this in the way that has become standard practice; that is to say, he withdrew his forces from the city to training camps outside Paris, weeded them out, re-constituted them and when they next went in there was no time for fraternisation to occur and the Commune was suppressed. It is only fair to point out that the Commune was, throughout, very much on the defensive. It could only have come into existence as a result of the military occupation of France by the Prussians, and was only possible as a form of government because of the power vacuum following the defeat of France and the long siege of Paris during the winter of 1870-1. The Prussians would not have allowed it to spread, but were happy to have the French incur the responsibility of suppressing it. So it was as a result of this experience that Engels wrote his famous remark in the introduction to *The Class Struggles in France, 1848-1850*—'let us have no illusions about it, a real victory of insurrection over the military in street fighting, a victory as between two armies, is one of the rarest exceptions.' (Marx and Engels, 1962, I, p. 130.)

Now the reason for this historical introduction is quite plain when one considers what had to be, logically speaking, the attitude of socialists in general to most of the important revolutionary movements in the latter half of the nineteenth century and the early party of the twentieth. It might have been logical to discard the idea of urban insurrection altogether, but there were powerful ideological reasons why this should not occur, and people who toyed with the idea of resorting to the coup on the one hand, or mass peasant uprisings on the other, were denounced. And the reason was quite simple: it would be extremely difficult for any uprising against an established government to claim mass support unless the mass support was visibly forthcoming. Once the example of mass support had been shown by the French Revolution, then its absence would, for the first time, have been noticeable.

The dilemmas are well indicated by the Comintern manual on urban insurrection published in English under the title of A. Neuberg, *Armed Insurrection* (Neuberg 1970). 'A. Neuberg' is a pseudonym for the Agitprop section of the Comintern under the direction of Togliatti, and the manual was prepared in 1928, and published in German, bearing the imprint of the City of Zurich and the imaginary publisher Otto Meyer. In fact, the only thing that was accurate about its original description is that it was about armed insurrection, and it was actually published in 1928. This seemed to be a particularly favourable moment for condensing the experience of the early 1920s into handbook form and making it available to the comrades for their instruction and it went out with an official seal of approval from the

Comintern, with, however, certain criticisms of its actual content.

It begins with two theoretical chapters written by Piatnitsky. Piatnitsky was then the organising secretary of the Comintern but was liquidated by Stalin during the 1930s. The theoretical chapters trace, in context, the Bolshevik directions for revolution. He was primarily concerned, firstly, with arguing, against Karl Kautsky the German Social Democrat leader, that only through violence could the bourgeois state be overthrown. Having picked up the quotation of Engels mentioned above, he then continued it according to what is supposed to be Engels' original text, which Eduard Bernstein had cut out.

Does this mean that in future street fighting will no longer play any role? Certainly not! It only means that conditions since 1848 have become far more unfavourable for civilian fighters and far more favourable for the military. In future, street fighting can therefore be victorious only if this disadvantageous situation is compensated for by other factors. Accordingly, it will occur more seldom in the beginning of a great revolution than in its further progress and will have to be undertaken with greater forces. These, however, may well then prefer, as in the whole great French Revolution or on September 4th and October 31st, 1870 in Paris, the open attack to the passive barricade tactics. [Neuberg 1970, pp. 35–6]

Three points here are obviously very important. To begin with, Piatnitsky argues that Engels held that street fighting would continue to be important, though because of the disadvantageous situation as against the regular military— by this time very much better armed than they had been back in 1848—this would have to be compensated for by other factors.

Secondly, Engels seems to argue that it was unlikely that urban insurrection would play a major role at the beginning of a great revolution rather than later on—in other words, a revolution would have to be initiated by some other means and then mass uprising would perform an important part in it. Such a formulation safeguarded the claim to a 'leading role' of the communist party.

And thirdly, that open attack was likely to be preferred to the passive barricade tactics. The interesting thing is that having taken note of this, the manual itself then proceeds to argue to a considerable extent to the contrary to the last two points, its authors preferring to follow what Lenin had since written in *Marx and Insurrection*:

To be successful, insurrection must rely, not on conspiracy, not upon a party, but upon the advanced class—that is the first point. Insurrection must rely upon a revolutionary upset of the people—that is the second point. Insurrection must rely upon that turning point in the history of the growing revolution when the activity of the advanced ranks of the people is at its height, and then the vacillations in the ranks of the enemy and the ranks of the weak half-hearted and irresolute friends of the revolution are strongest—that is the third point. And these three conditions for raising the question of insurrection distinguish Marxism from Blanquism. [Neuberg 1970, p. 42]

Lenin is here expounding the distinction between subjective and objective conditions for an urban insurrection, which becomes crucial. Lenin argues that although it is possible to take the subjective decision to make the decision to place insurrection on the agenda, before it can be placed on the agenda the objective conditions have to be correct. This presents two problems. If the objective conditions are right but the decision is not taken to proceed with insurrection, obviously the revolution cannot follow. Lenin himself claimed that a revolutionary situation had been present in Russia in 1905. It had also, he claimed, been present in Russia in 1859–61 and 1879–80. Elsewhere, he claimed that it had been present in Germany in the 1860s, but he is not very specific exactly when. On all these occasions, he says, there was a revolutionary situation but the revolution did not materialise. If, on the other hand, the objective conditions are not right and the decision is taken to proceed with insurrection, the revolution will be forestalled. Neuberg gives examples of two early incidents which he terms Blanquist, that is, incidents that were carried out when the time was *not* ripe: the rising of August 1870 in Paris (before the Commune) and the July Days in Russia in 1917. On both these occasions, he says, the situation was not ripe. To go ahead and prepare an insurrection when the time is not ripe is to be Putschist—to try and carry out a mere military putsch, or coup. Later Putschist attempts, Neuberg argues, were the Revolt of March 1921 in Germany, the Reval insurrection in 1924 in Estonia, and the second Shanghai insurrection of February 1927.

Assessing the situation becomes clearly a major problem for a bolshevik wishing to carry out an armed insurrection who wishes, first of all, to find out when the time is right. So the next four chapters of the manual are chapters of case studies, dealing in turn with the Reval uprising (the reader will not find Reval on a modern map: it is now called Talinn), the Hamburg uprising, the Canton insurrection and the three Shanghai insurrections. The reason for the detail and interest in the Chinese examples is because Ho Chi Minh (or, as he was then called, Nyguen Thanh) was one of the authors of the manual.

There follow three chapters on political preparation for the insurrection and two chapters by Tukhachevsky on the military tactics to be followed. The political problem basically revolves around the military question—and a legitimate criticism made by the Comintern of its own manual was that it concerned itself too much with the military and not enough with the political.

An entire long chapter, to begin with, is devoted to the subversion of the military. The army, it says, is the key element in the organisation of the state. Upon its stability and its general condition depend the stability of the state as a whole. It points out that the military was not adequately subverted at Reval where, indeed, the insurrectionists made a number of other mistakes including not being ready in time. Worse, communists had wasted the opportunities they had had for subverting the military in Germany, where the military under the Weimar Constitution was unusually open to penetration. Normally, as we have already seen, military forces are protected to a considerable extent against penetration, and in any case are retrained in barracks so that subversion is very difficult to achieve. The manual argues that the reason why this has not been adequately done is that their people are waiting for revolution to happen spontaneously in the aftermath of a great war and they fail to realise, they say, that revolutionary situations also arise in times of 'peace' (quotation marks in original—Neuberg 1970, p. 153). And the military, they suggest, can be easily subverted by two means: firstly, the use of situations which are, in fact, specifically military in content; in other words, where the military have been defeated, and that rankles. And secondly, by supporting what they call the partial demands of the military, which will stimulate the class struggle in the army. This is done by asking for better pay, better living conditions, etc. At the same time, the manual warns the comrades who are engaged in this action, first of all that it is extremely dangerous but, for that reason must in fact be stepped up, not down; and secondly, that the bourgeoisie will do anything, simply anything to avoid revolution, including getting the soldiers drunk in order to keep them in line—so subversion will be very difficult. Interestingly enough, it devotes precisely two paragraphs to the party infiltration of the police, despite the fact that it observes that there was considerable sympathy in police circles for the party in Germany in 1923, when the police of course were highly politicised and there was a social democratic government in Germany.

Subversion of the military is only one part of the preparatory organisation recommended by the manual, the other part is the organisation of the proletarian force, the Red Guard. Here, the first problem is getting hold of recruits. Neuberg stresses that, as Lenin advises, the Red Guard can only be formed when the seizure of power is 'on the immediate agenda' (Neuberg 1970, p. 172). The bourgeoisie will not allow the creation of a Red Guard while the situation has not yet become one of civil war and they will endeavour to prevent it by every means possible. Then, even if a skeleton Red Guard is set up with cadres, it will still take months to make it into a really effective fighting force. Yet, it may at the same time (and this is the intrinsic paradox of the book's approach to armed insurrection) have to take the brunt of the fighting until the bourgeois army is disarmed or begins to waver.

The second problem is that of armaments. Clearly the bourgeoisie (for which read 'the established government') is not going to permit people to arm themselves unless they think they are on their side. Yet it is Lenin's view that the insurrectionists must immediately arm, and must start building up stores of arms as early as possible.

The contingents . . . [Lenin says] must arm themselves as best they can (rifles, revolvers, bombs, knives, knuckledusters, sticks, rags soaked in kerosene for starting fires, ropes or rope ladders, shovels for building barricades, pyroxylin cartridges, barbed wire, nails against cavalry, etc., etc.) Under no circumstances should they wait for help from other sources, from above, from the outside; they must procure everything themselves. [Neuberg 1970, p. 177.]

Where from, Lenin, and the manual, do not say, but in modern times the competition between suppliers has become more intense than ever before.

The next problem is, how are the rebels trained to use them? And this really is the nub of the question, not satisfactorily resolved by the manual. If you want to train people for urban insurrection, it believes, they should disguise themselves as members of an ex-servicemen's organisation or drill in secret or something like that. And really very little adequate guidance is given as to how this might be done.

Instead, then, they go on to the military problems. These two chapters are written by Marshal Tukhachevsky who was, at that time, Second in Command of the Red Army. As is well known, Tukhachevsky disappeared in the course of the spectacular show trial of 1937, but was posthumously rehabilitated (for what that is worth) by Khrushchev. It is particularly interesting to find that Tukhachevsky diverges completely from the idea that armed insurrection will only be used in the *later* stages of a revolution. He, in fact, stresses from the beginning that the struggle will take place in the cities.

In the first period of this open civil war, the struggle will take place principally in the cities, i.e. it will take the form of street battles— which, of course, will differ in nature and duration according to circumstances. It is upon the outcome of the battle in this period, and upon the speed with which the proletariat succeeds in creating a sufficient number of Red Army units in fighting trim, that will depend to a very considerable extent on the outcome of the struggle to consolidate the revolution and to extend it territorially. [Neuberg 1970, p. 185]

Tukhachevsky, therefore, takes as given, the existence of armed insurrection from the very first moment of the revolt. Then he goes on to discuss its distinctive problems. There are four principal ones: firstly, in urban fighting there is no frontline. This can cut both ways because a regular soldier may not be any more happy in the city than the army of the proletariat. Secondly, the army of the proletariat will not be ready; the 'regular army of the proletariat' is created, and must be created in the course of the struggle for power. Thirdly, on the other hand, insurrection modifies, and indeed subverts the army of the ruling class (the established government).

Lastly, he argues that because they are making use of untrained amateur soldiers the communists have both their advantages and disadvantages; they have to achieve superiority at the start, avoid the defensive, and provide a series of continuous successes. If they do this, the untrained nature of their fighting force will give them extra fighting power—in other words, they will not realise the fantastic odds that they are overcoming.

Specific suggestions then follow; there are a large number and the manual is very detailed. It is clear that Tukhachevsky had thought out the problem of urban insurrection extremely clearly, and the only problem was how it would actually be put into practice. Firstly, armed workers (he points out) could very easily take over all the secondary targets like banks, workplaces, railway stations and installations that do not actually need armed fighting men to take them over, because they are not normally guarded. Secondly, then, he points out that the forces of the government can be disorientated by picking off the leaders, and he goes into considerable discussion to try and prove that this is not a terrorist action and therefore reprehensible, but is in fact quite Leninist; that one should concentrate on picking off the leaders and killing them as quickly as possible. This seems to account for the Indonesian examples.

Thirdly, at the start, surprise is necessary. This can be achieved by detailed reconnaissance of the circumstances and by preparing an adequate fighting force for the tasks in hand. At Reval, for example, there was detailed reconnaissance but its execution failed. At the officer cadet academy they succeeded in disarming those on the ground floor, but apparently the force which was meant to disarm the first floor did not turn up in time, and the cadets on the first floor were able to hold out. The trouble was that, having had this slight setback, the revolutionaries failed to change their plans. Instead of swarming through the building with the forces they then had at their disposal, they fell back disheartened, withdrew and lost an important stronghold.

Neuberg points out that timing is extremely important and should always be set in advance. To rely on signals such as cannon shot or rockets or suchlike to launch a revolt, as the bolsheviks did with the *Aurora* in 1917, is a great mistake because people are unlikely either to see them, to hear them, or to pay any attention to them. Apparently, in the Bulgarian Insurrection in 1923 this actually happened. Someone was supposed to fire a cannon as a signal for the rising. The gun went off but people in one part of the city heard it while people in the other part did not and the result was disaster (Neuberg 1970, p. 211).

Those who think that there are no male chauvinists in the Soviet Union may note Tukhachevsky's observation: 'Experience shows that there are great advantages in using women and children for reconnaissance work, and that all missions of a less complicated kind should be entrusted to them.' (Ibid., pp. 234–5.)

This section of the manual concludes with the discussion of defensive actions, on the realistic grounds that the proletariat may not, even given these instructions, succeed in carrying out successfully an urban insurrection, but it can all be used as training for the future. Clearly, even Marshals of the Soviet Union treat their forces with the same kind of disregard for life that generals do in other countries. Tukhachevsky told them cheerfully how to build barricades, how successfully to throw bombs at tanks, dig holes in the ground, and stick it out for the sake of the cause to the final hour. The manual concludes with some words from Ho Chi Minh on how to prepare a peasant uprising, the argument for this being that it is a very useful thing to have going on in the background, while the Red Guard is occupied seizing the cities.

This manual was published, as noted above, in 1928. Since then there have been several urban insurrections but practically none of them have been successful. This suggests that there is something wrong with the idea of urban insurrection altogether. By an odd coincidence, the interesting examples are in states with communist governments, which reinforces the view that it was not by pure accident that Tukhachevsky and the old bolsheviks who were behind the writing of this manual were among the first people liquidated in 1936-8. The most interesting examples since Stalin's death are the Hungarian uprising of 1956, the risings in Poland in 1944, 1953 and 1970 (the last of which, of course, was successful in the overthrow of Mr Gomulka), and the East German rising of 1953. All these are examples in which there was large-scale mass uprising, where the manual workers played an important part, and played very much the Tukhachevsky way—taking over the secondary targets and indeed, even making use of blasting charges, pits for tanks, gasoline bombs and all the other things that Lenin long ago suggested workers might use if they wanted to take political power. About the only thing they did not seem to use were pyroxylin cartridges.

There have also been a number of abortive communist revolts in other countries, the most interesting of which is the series that occurred in Indonesia: the rising of 1928 (the same year as the Tukhachevsky manual was published); the Madiun uprising of 1948; and the abortive uprising (Gestapu) of 1965, mentioned above.

Now as a rising, as I have shown, this last was a complete disaster. The interesting thing is that, looked at in the light of the Comintern manual, it fulfilled to a nicety the kind of conditions which the manual laid down. The insurrection was pre-planned; its promoters had a contingency plan set to operate; there was one specific signal, which was to be the death of Sukarno. (They obviously forgot that it would not necessarily be advisable to use this kind of signal since not everyone would have heard of it. Besides, Sukarno might not even oblige them by dying—which he did not.) Thirdly, the insurrectionists struck directly at the main leaders of the government, mainly the military leaders, in a successful effort to disorientate the other side. They ruthlessly slaughtered them, according to the Tukhachevsky instructions, and their bodies were thrown down a well. And lastly, the revolt was concentrated in Jakarta, although obviously a mass uprising in Indonesia (then almost entirely a rural country) involved something much more widespread than that. In fact, the mass uprising which eventually occurred was an anti-communist uprising and it resulted in the fearful massacres of late 1965 in Indonesia when some 500,000 died.

Obviously there is a fundamental theoretical problem for a Marxist, as to whether he is going to persist with this very dangerous technique which has proved so disastrously unsuccessful in so many situations; whether he adopts a putschist strategy, or whether he goes for guerrilla warfare. Putschism in a sense was the choice of Lenin himself. In October 1917 he took political power by an organised coup in which the urban insurrection element was, practically speaking, minimised. He tells the Central Committee, after the plans are made, of using the existing military forces, many of whom are regular army units, that had already been subverted. The alternative is to go to the other extreme and adopt the guerrilla way—the Maoist, Castro, Guevara or whatever version, according to taste.

7. Diplomacy and revolution

At the point at which revolutions affect other states, or are liable to be affected by them, particular importance attaches to the formal structure of international diplomacy, and the agents by whom it is carried on.

As we have already noted, the European states have, in the past four centuries, taken a leading role in setting up a world-wide system of diplomacy. In the present century this has been extended in two ways: on the one hand its formal structure has been extended to encompass the world system, including the multitude of new states. On the other, it has been extended beyond its original basic concept as an instrument of negotiation between pairs of states into a multilateral system of legal ideas and procedures. Though these fall far short of a world system of government, such ideas and rules are in general observed by the vast majority of states most of the time. They do so for four main reasons: self-advantage, habit, prestige and fear of reprisal (cf. Holsti 1967, p. 412). It is precisely this relationship of custom and habit that is threatened by sudden political changes within the state.

Diplomacy is the conduct of negotiations between states in the international system according to customary practices formulated to assist in securing peaceful agreement. Other writers have offered other definitions, one particularly attractive one being that of Satow:

Diplomacy is the application of intelligence and tact to the conduct of official relations between the government of independent states, extending sometimes also to their relations with vassal states; or, more briefly still, the conduct of business between states by peaceful means. [Satow 1957, p. 1.]

The official business of doing so is carried on by specially trained officials known generally as 'diplomats', and collectively as a state's 'diplomatic service'.

The term 'diplomatic service' came into existence as late as

1787. Like 'diplomat' and 'diplomacy' it is derived from the word 'diploma', meaning an official letter empowering the bearer to negotiate on behalf of his government and in return assuring him of his personal safety and freedom while he did so. In this sense the practice of diplomacy is much older than the word. Machiavelli, to take a famous example, was a diplomat, for he conducted foreign policy and was engaged in negotiations between states. And it was in fact at the time that he was living, the Italian Renaissance, that there first evolved in Europe a system of permanent representatives stationed in the capitals of other states to negotiate with their rulers on a full-time basis. The Venetians, who played a leading role in this process, were primarily interested in the protection and extension of trade. Although it was for this purpose that diplomacy was invented, in practice the day-to-day workings of trade were entrusted to officials called 'consuls' who, with the consular services of which they formed part, had a lower status in international eyes.

Diplomacy evolved in a world of monarchical states, and its customs reflect its origins. One ruler could not concede precedence to another. Diplomacy grew up, therefore, on the basis of an equal exchange of representatives, called ambassadors or ministers, between two rulers. Each was regarded as representing his ruler, who as an anointed ruler (Christian or otherwise) was protected from physical harm by religious fear as well as by legal sanction. During his mission, therefore, he was personally immune from arrest or attack, and his house and belongings were exempt from search or confiscation. The beginning of his mission was marked, on arrival, by his formal reception by the head of state, at which he presented the official letters of credence which were the proof of his status and powers.

The operation of the entire system depended on the mutual recognition of one another by the states concerned. Once that was achieved, each had an interest in maintaining the links that had been established, and though in the first instance the Venetians had encountered particular problems in relations with Turkey, from which for one reason or another some of their early ambassadors failed to return, in due course even Turkey, though not a Christian state, accepted the value of diplomacy. From that time onwards the main problems in the extension and maintenance of the system came from states that had undergone revolutionary changes, and who therefore regarded themselves as no longer being bound by the rules of a system to whose growth they had not contributed (Falk 1962). History shows that these problems are not in any way new to the twentieth century, and that some of these earlier experiences have still something to teach us about the nature of diplomacy and of the international system.

Firstly, there is the problem of recognition. A state that changes its form of government has, if it is to continue to deal with other states, first of all to be recognised by them. Until a government is recognised by its peers it can play no formal role. A new government is therefore in an exceptionally vulnerable position to pressure from other states, who can make use of its desire for recognition to try to force it to behave in a way that suits their interests. If it does not, their continued failure to recognise it may well have no significant effect on its internal politics, but it can and does act to reduce its influence in world affairs. Thus, the fact that the United States withheld recognition from the People's Republic of China from 1949 to 1973 had no adverse effect on China internally, but it precluded it from a full role in international affairs and by corollary the United States was also able to prevent it from being admitted to the United Nations, where it would otherwise have been able to take up its permanent seat in the Security Council, with the right of veto. Most states seek recognition, which is not to say that they cannot survive without recognition, and of course China was gradually successful in obtaining recognition from a large number of states before it was ever admitted to the United Nations. But basically a state is handicapped in its international relations by not being admitted into the formal system, and the interesting thing is that in the case of the Soviet Union, for example, who, after all, came into existence on the platform of the complete overthrow of the existing order, had by 1922 effectively accepted the mechanism of international diplomacy, for the simple reason that there really is nothing else even now to take its place.

To be recognised by other states and to gain admittance into this system, a government has, first of all, to observe their customs; in other words, to accommodate itself to the existing framework of diplomacy. Thus, for example, G. V. Chicherin, the Soviet People's Commissar for Foreign Affairs from 1918 to 1930, found himself in a tailcoat, by 1922, so that he could get into international conferences and be dressed like all the others; because he knew that if he did not turn up looking like the others he was not going to be able to negotiate on an equal basis.

Secondly, the incoming government has to avoid giving cause for offence. The usual way of giving such offence is by cancelling the debts of past governments and the Russian government, of course, did that. But it did something very much more offensive, by publishing the secret Czarist archives, including the text of the secret treaties that had been made by Russia during the Great War, describing how the allies were going to carve up the map of Europe, once they had the chance.

One of the characteristics of a revolutionary 'style' is frequently the rejection of traditional diplomatic methods and techniques, on the grounds that they are 'loaded', that they represent the features of an international order that a revolutionary state opposes. As Spanier puts it:

A revolutionary state—such as the Soviet Union after World War II— is a state at war. It rejects the social and economic structure of the traditional states who dominate the state system because it views this prevailing order as the source of injustice and war. [Spanier 1967]

Such states use international agencies not for the resolution of disputes in a peaceful manner, but for propaganda, agitation and intimidation. Hence they may, as the communist countries have traditionally done, make extensive use of insulting epithets and abusive accusations against their political opponents or, as we have already noticed, make use of negotiations as a cover for the more or less surreptitious use of force. Interestingly enough they have rarely—as the Iranian Revolutionary Government did in 1979–81— rejected the conventions of the diplomatic system entirely to the extent of abusing the persons of diplomats accredited to them, still less using them as hostages for demands on foreign governments; though from 1967 onwards hostage-taking became routine practice among terrorist movements with revolutionary intent, as a means of publicising their own cause and often securing large ransom sums or the release of valuable members of their groups. In these events diplomatic personnel, for a time, became the prime targets, as the individuals most specifically identified with the policies of the governments they served.

This is particularly sad since, whatever its shortcomings, diplomacy is a prime factor in the struggle for peace. Whatever else it may be, diplomacy is not war.

War may be the continuation of foreign policy by other means, but it is not just the same thing as diplomacy. Moreover, the existence of a state of war does not put an end to diplomacy, for without diplomacy war cannot be brought to an end. It is one of the most respected principles of international law as well as domestic law that the mere seizure of territory or property by force does not confer a right to it. Only by diplomatic agreement, therefore, can the arrangements be made by which the victors secure their gains or settle their losses.

In order for this to happen, as already noted, diplomats have to have protection. Since this protection is supposed to be the same as that enjoyed by the sovereigns they represent, the natural question arises: 'How far does a sovereign who has been deposed enjoy the protection of the international system?' In theory, not at all. As Satow says, 'A sovereign who has been deposed by his people, or who has abdicated, and whose deposition or abdication has been recognised by other states, and a president of a republic whose term of office has expired or who has been overthrown by a revolution, enjoys no immunities' (Satow 1957, p. 7). But in practice such an individual is usually treated with courtesy by other states, at least for a period of time following his fall, by the unspoken custom of the 'trade union of rulers'. And in Latin America since the late nineteenth century politicians generally have been able to avail themselves of the diplomatic immunity of the legations or embassies of other countries to take refuge from revolt and pass subsequently into exile in safety, from which they not infrequently return in triumph at the next turn of Fortune's wheel. Even elsewhere it is certainly not customary to kill rulers who have been overthrown. It is usual to let them go into exile. But there is then a very delicate problem for other states as to what they do with the rulers who have arrived in exile. How do they treat them? They are, in fact, technically only private citizens, but usually for diplomatic reasons hosts feel they have to treat them with a certain amount of care in case they might suddenly find themselves back in office the next day, when a public snub might be rather embarrassing, as in the case of the United States and the ex-Shah of Iran.

We can now return to the question of immunity for ambassador. On the appointment of the minister for foreign foreign countries is in fact the minister for foreign affairs (MFA) who will normally conduct business with the visiting ambassador. On the appointment of the minister of foreign affairs he notifies the members of the diplomatic corps resident in his capital, and receives the heads of missions in order of precedence, which nowadays means the order in which they have been appointed. All normal communications are addressed to him, bar one; the one exception is the Letter of Credence which is presented when a new ambassador arrives, which is addressed to the head of state.

It is the responsibility of the minister for foreign affairs, reciprocal with that of his opposite number in the other country, to guarantee the privileges and immunities of ambassadors even in time of civil disturbance. Diplomacy does not easily recognise the existence of a state of civil disturbance and therefore if care is not taken to protect ambassadors and diplomatic personnel generally, this may be taken as evidence by foreign countries that the government is incapable of governing, in which case they are then at liberty to recognise another government. As Satow again says:

When a civil war or revolution breaks out, agents dispatched to foreign countries by the opponents of the hitherto constituted government ought not to be officially received until the new state of things has assumed a permanent character and given rise to the formation of a new *de facto* government. The fact that a party in the state during a civil

war has been recognised as a belligerent involves no right to be diplomatically represented abroad. [Satow 1957, p. 119, sec. 198]

So when a civil war or revolution breaks out in a foreign
country the representatives of the pre-existing government
must continue to be treated as being such until the MFA is
formally notified that that government has been overthrown.
Conversely, in a country where disturbance breaks out the
minister for foreign affairs *remains* responsible for the safety
of diplomatic personnel until he himself is actually overthrown.

Now, supposing a civil war situation arises (as in Spain
between 1936 and 1939), what is the status in international
relations of the contending party, which I shall call the
opposition? The answer is: technically, it has no status—a
foreign power cannot recognise it diplomatically without
automatically breaking off recognition of the existing government. In the case of secession, as in Bangladesh, for example,
recognition of the government of Bangladesh gave rise
immediately to severance of relations by Pakistan. Any
country may, in theory, at any time, if it wishes, sever
diplomatic relations with any other, but it is in fact regarded
as a cause of offence to do so. This may not matter if, as in
1962, the government of Guatemala, on account of the
Belize question, decides no longer to recognise the existence
of the United Kingdom: the United Kingdom staggered
along regardless. But it may matter a great deal if a very small
country, contiguous to a large one, is not recognised by the
government of that larger country; this may give rise to
considerable *internal* embarrassment. Because the fact that it
has not been recognised means that if the existing government is threatened, then no holds are barred, and the normal
rules and decencies of diplomacy need not be observed. This
is termed *non*-recognition—the ability to put moral pressure
on an incumbent government by saying 'We do not regard
you as having the right to exist'.

The status of belligerency which Satow refers to, is a
different question. It is open to a government when a
country is in a state of civil war, to recognise the opposition
party as belligerents. This does not imply diplomatic

recognition and it does not entitle them to representation, even if they want it. But it does entitle them to conduct certain kinds of commercial business, particularly buying and selling arms, which they then find extremely convenient. So to recognise a state of belligerency is to recognise the actual existence of a state of war. It is not to pronounce moral judgement, although it tends to be regarded as a sign that perhaps the insurgents have a point. And 'foreign states may negotiate with the agents of such belligerents informally, to provide for the safety of their subjects and the property of their subjects resident within the territory under the sway of such a party.' (Oppenheim 1952, I, p. 693, sec. 362.)

During the continuance of civil war or revolution the diplomatist on the spot may often have to intervene on behalf of his own countrymen, with the insurgents in possession, but he will do this personally and unofficially until his government recognises a new power which has been set up and, if necessary, send him new credentials. As long as recognition does not take place, the diplomatic agent previously accredited continues to represent the head of the state which appointed him. [Satow 1957, p. 119, sec. 198]

Hence, unless a decision is taken to end recognition, the incumbent ambassador of the foreign power continues to represent his state until *either* he is withdrawn *or* notification is given that the state of affairs at home is changed, *or* a decision is taken on whether to recognise the changed state of affairs in the other country.

Now the mere act of changing an ambassador always implies new credentials. One cannot, therefore, replace a diplomatic agent under such conditions without formally according recognition to the new regime. Secondly, however:

There is no fixed method of according recognition to a new government which has assumed office as a result of a revolutionary outbreak. Any form of notification suffices for the purpose, or any act on the part of a state which is consistent only with such recognition. [Satow 1957, p. 120, sec. 199, see also Nicolson 1963, pp. 190–1]

That is to say: if one sends a new ambassador, this is consistent only with recognising the new government. If one sends a diplomatic note that too is consistent only with recognition

—in other words, if one is not going to recognise the government one cannot send it diplomatic notes.

Recognition can, therefore, serve as a bargaining point with new revolutionary governments. In 1910 Britain delayed the recognition of the Portuguese Republic until it had called a general election, which gave the majority to the Republicans, and, secondly, altered their draft Constitution, to permit Anglican worship. In the case of Greece in 1924 the British Government accorded recognition only after the new republic had been approved by a plebiscite. It is often regarded as being overbearing of large powers to do this but in fact in diplomatic practice it is perfectly respectable.

A mere change of ministry does not, however, affect diplomatic recognition. It is a very moot point as to whether it is even necessary to accord recognition to a person who has come to power as a result of a military coup, even when he is an executive head of state. For example, in the case of Chile and Ecuador in 1925, and Peru, Argentina and Brazil in 1930, when they had military coups, the British representative was simply instructed to inform the government concerned 'that the British government considered their diplomatic relations between the two countries were in no way affected by the change of government.' And that in itself is sufficient. And by doing that, the British Government avoided the embarrassment of having to recognise them officially.

In the case of the Soviet Union in 1924, however, Britain recognised the government of the Soviet Union as the 'de jure rulers of those territories of the old Russian Empire which recognised their authority.' This is very interesting, because of the vast difference between de facto and de jure recognition. De facto recognition means only recognising that the government is effectively in control of the country, and British practice is always to recognise governments when they are effectively in control of their respective countries. In the case of the Soviet Union, Britain not only recognised the Soviet government as the de facto rulers, but also de jure. To recognise them de jure means that they have legitimacy. This is a very important difference because it means that the government according recognition accepts the right of the new government to exist. Recognising a government de jure therefore means that, technically, recognition cannot be withdrawn—although in practice it can if circumstances have changed.

Finally, the immunity of the diplomatic representative is not affected by any of these changes. As long as he is still there with his letters of credence from his original government, he is affected neither by the demise of the government to whom he is accredited nor of the government from which he is accredited. A diplomatic representative in a foreign capital who has been accredited by a government that has now been overthrown by force, even in time of war, is still entitled to full immunity until he is safely back in his own country (Satow 1957, p. 192, sec. 317). And diplomatic immunity applies also in those countries the agent passes through on his way.

Now what, we might easily ask, do you do with the ambassador of a foreign country who conspires against the country to which he is accredited? The first thing is that ambassadors today usually take enormous care to avoid being caught doing this, and therefore there are no recent instances that we can actually prove. It seems customary to entrust these important matters, for example, in the Russian case, to the Third Secretary's chauffeur who is in fact a colonel in the KGB. The ambassador knows nothing about this and it would be very embarrassing indeed if he did— he takes good care that he does not. Occasionally, ambassadors have used diplomatic influence against incumbent governments—for example, the United States Ambassador John Puerifoy, in Greece, and in Guatemala. But that is diplomatically respectable. Ambassadors are allowed to do that; what they are not allowed to do is to promote a military conspiracy against the government to whom they are accredited. In fact there is no evidence that Puerifoy did this; though in the latter country he did take advantage of a military conspiracy to see that the government that he wanted was put in power.

So the historical instances of conspiracy are now remote. Two are mentioned by Satow (pp. 118-9). In the year 1716 Count Gryllenborg, who was the Swedish minister in London, was engaged in a Jacobite conspiracy to depose King

George I. He was arrested and his papers were seized. Immediately the Swedish government received the news, they ordered the arrest of the British minister in Stockholm, and later the two were exchanged. Curiously though, in 1718, the Count Cellemare, who was the Spanish ambassador in Paris, was engaged—it seems to have been the custom of the time—in conspiracy against the Regent of France, in favour of the King of Spain who had a claim to the throne of France. He was promptly arrested by the French government. The news, however, reached the French ambassador in Madrid before it reached the government there. He set off post-haste for the frontier, and, as it happened, managed to get over the frontier safely before the Spanish government could catch him. On this occasion there was no hostage to exchange, but in fact the French government very diplomatically decided they would simply return Cellemare to Spain, and they did so in circumstances of considerable ignominy.

Diplomatic agents, whether actually engaged in conspiracy or not, can and often are expelled as *persona non grata* to the incumbent regime. No reasons need be given as to why a person is *persona non grata*, and in fact, great care is taken in appointing diplomats to ensure beforehand that they are *persona grata*. This is done by taking soundings and getting the agreement of the government to whom the diplomat is to be accredited. For example, Mr Harold Wilson welcoming the new President of the United States in 1969, found his Foreign Secretary was due to send them a new ambassador. Incredibly, the new ambassador who had been picked was John Freeman, a former editor of the *New Statesman* who had spent a good many enthusiastic years criticising President Nixon, and might well not be *persona grata* in Washington. Nixon, who was gifted with a sense of humour, did accept this appointment, but it is scarcely likely that his past actually helped the ambassador to discharge his duties. Certainly this is very unlikely to happen with most other governments. Normally a person who had engaged in this kind of activity would be *persona non grata* and the government would simply indicate their preference for some other appointment to be made. This advice is always followed for obvious reasons. There is no point in appointing a diplomat who is going to be regarded as undiplomatic.

The problem for us is that when there is a revolutionary government in power, almost any diplomat may become undiplomatic. On the other hand, revolutionary governments in times of great revolutions are so arrogant that they do not care whether their ambassadors are received or not; they reject the existing processes of diplomacy, along with their predecessors in government.

The first example is when the English parliament executed King Charles I. Its ambassador to Spain, who was an admiral and given to the blunt speech of his type, arrived at Cadiz and promptly proceeded to make a public speech in which he said, among other things:

> With the example afforded by London all kingdoms will annihilate tyranny and become republics. England has done so already; France is following in her wake; and as the natural gravity of the Spaniards renders them somewhat slower in their operations, it will take Spain ten years to make the revolution. [Thompson and Padover 1963, p. 83]

Needless to say, he was not welcomed by the Spanish government and was in fact requested to leave.

Later, when Cromwell took over the reins of office and brought them under his own control, he became a forerunner of the most distinctive characteristic of revolutionary diplomacy in that he set up a secret agency for the conduct of foreign policy. In fact, he conducted his foreign policy officially and unofficially through the same man, John Thurloe, the Secretary of State. He was prepared to spend up to £70,000 annually on obtaining intelligence at foreign courts. Specifically, he would pay up to £1,000 annually to buy good information in Rome, and in fact bought a cardinal for the purpose. (It may seem a little improbable that the government of a puritan regime like Cromwell's should have managed to suborn a cardinal but in fact cardinals were going quite cheap in 1650.) What defeated everyone else about Cromwellian foreign policy (and it is a recurrent feature of revolutionary regimes) was its secrecy. It was so secret that even the Venetian ambassador to Madrid, Sagredo, was unable at first to find out what was going on. In those days, if the Venetian ambassador did not know what was going on, no one knew what was going on. The reports of the Venetian Embassy, with all the money that they had at their disposal were second to none, and they had the finest diplomatic and intelligence nets in Europe. They got very upset when in the end they discovered what the English were up to, for they were really descending to thoroughly low tricks. 'To discover the affairs of others they do not employ ambassadors, but use spies, as less conspicuous, making use of men of spirit but without rank, unlikely to be noticed,' the Venetian complained. (Ibid., p. 85.)

This is the key to the operation of revolutionary diplomacy, which tends to make use, not of the formal machinery of diplomatic intercourse, but of a separate and distinct net. And in the tremendously status-ridden societies, even—dare one say it—of today, the men of spirit but without rank are the people who are able to pick up the good information. And they are also the people who are able to buy up the information they require or to make the necessary negotiations in delicate parts of the state. Cromwell was therefore one of the first to separate the function of intelligence from diplomacy which up to that time had really been one and the same thing.

Another great Englishman, if he may be described as such, who was also a pioneer in this field, was William III (1689–1702). William was very very short of cash, and he found, contrary to popular belief, that the less cash he had the better his foreign policy was. Diplomacy was fearfully expensive in those days, and it did not bring in very much goodwill either, because one always offended more people than one actually made friends of. William set the tone of eighteenth-century diplomacy, which in fact persisted right into the nineteenth century, by using few permanent missions but a great many agents engaged in promoting trade—again a product of a revolutionary situation.

Thirdly, in the time of the French Convention, one finds the sudden reappearance of intelligence and unofficial agents. During 1793 alone, at the height of the Terror, the Government spent on spies the sum of 1,300,000 livres. (The livre was then worth about ten pence in English money.) They spent this on a centre of espionage in the Ministry of Foreign Affairs, which reported weekly to the ministerial conference and then to the Committee of Public Safety and to the Paris Commune. They paid special attention to foreigners resident in France, who were the subject of great suspicion at all times. They thought they were probably enemies of liberty and engaged in plotting against the regime and none more so than Gouverneur Morris, the Minister of the United States, whom they identified as the greatest enemy of liberty because he was not very keen on the public execution of aristocrats.

Washington's coolness towards the French Revolution was known to the French and in order to try and represent the true feelings of French revolutionary government to the people of the United States, they decided they would send a trusted minister to the United States. Citizen Genet arrived in Philadelphia in exactly the same spirit as the English revolutionary agents of Cromwell's time, and proceeded to make a series of speeches to the people, inciting them to overthrow President Washington, whom he regarded as an enemy of liberty. He was promptly expelled as an agent and of course the French revolutionaries could never see why. The name of Chauvelin, who was the French minister to London is, of course, rather more familiar from the works of Baroness Orczy, and he too was engaged in a great number of very interesting activities. The Convention, however, was again (exactly like the English) not very interested in the effect of their foreign agents. It was considered necessary 'to abandon for a time the principles of scrupulousness in dealing with enemies who are unscrupulous, or rather, as ferocious, as ours are' (ibid., p. 184). All means are good against an ungodly race.

Lastly, we can compare the attitude of Russia, after 1922 the Soviet Union. By this time intelligence is by general consent clearly separated from diplomacy. So the official foreign ministry of the Soviet Union, the People's Commisariat of Foreign Affairs, was actually charged with very low level duties, primarily conducting trade negotiations. The intelligence function was, on the other hand, placed under the same organ as the secret police which they used for internal affairs, though a separate intelligence bureau for the military was established.

Even more important was the setting-up of the Comintern, the Communist International Information Bureau. The Comintern organisation was from the beginning an organ of the Soviet government. Its duty was to promote Soviet foreign policy aims abroad by conducting revolutionary movements in other countries (Black and Thornton 1964), and it was, as was noted in Chapter 6, appropriately staffed with experts in these activities. Chicherin, the People's Commissar for Foreign Affairs, dealt with trade, conferences, passports and treaties; in other words, fairly low-level activities. However, like all previous revolutionary regimes, they did use the embassies as a cover for their covert activities, so while the ambassador was busy being nice to the bourgeoisie the chauffeurs were busy subverting them and getting secrets about the atom bomb. The general rule therefore seems to be, the more drastic the change made by revolution in the diplomatic structure, the more likely it is to engage in unconventional diplomacy.

The most important thing is that a major revolution of this kind almost always involves a major diplomatic upheaval for one specific reason—it means a reversal of alliances. The revolutionary overthrow of the government means that by definition the new government will not be *persona grata* to those who are already allied to the old government. And a reversal of alliance is therefore necessary and implicates the new government in having to defend its own position in a potentially hostile world. It is bound to be all the more forthright in rejecting the current world order in the most serious of all emergencies, when it is itself seriously menaced and even attacked by counter-revolutionary forces in league with the governments of neighbouring states. This was the case in the three historical examples we have just noted: the English, French and Russian Revolutions. In recent times it has also been notable in the case of Cuba, attacked by the United States in 1961; Angoloa, where the counter-revolutionary UNITA government was supported by the physical intrusion of South African troops; and Nicaragua, where the Reagan administration has supported, armed and financed the counter-revolutionary forces operating against it from neighbouring Honduras.

It cannot be stressed too often that one of the most dangerous things a great power can do is to intervene militarily in a revolutionary situation. If the revolutionary government is not effectively crushed, opposition to it immediately becomes treason and may be punished as such; in any case, the almost inevitable result is the radicalisation of the revolutionary government and the destruction of the political moderates. Aid and intervention, however, are such a complex subject that they will be dealt with on their own in the next chapter.

8. Aid and intervention

We must first define 'intervention' and 'aid'. Some writers take the cynical view that aid is what *we* do—and intervention is what *they* do. Others make the more specific point, that aid refers specifically to material facilities and intervention to the dispatch of personnel. This in turn implies that intervention is one of at least two things: *diplomatic intervention*, in which an ambassador or other diplomatic agent makes a particular move in a specific situation which is designed to affect the internal politics of the country concerned, or *military intervention*, in which a state sends in troops in an effort to change the government or regime of another country.

It is becoming fashionable to use the word 'intervention' in an extremely loose way, but a third aspect which has been distinguished in the recent literature, *economic intervention*, is of particular importance. This is supposed to refer to the processes of economic penetration of a state by foreign companies or by international corporations. But economic intervention is rather an unattractive concept because, although there is no doubt about the existence of economic structures penetrating other states, they do so in a continuous process; it is not something that happens at a specific moment. Yet the word 'intervention' implies a process of *coming between* two contending parties in such a way as to adjust the balance of advantage between them (cf. Little 1975, p. 6). When we talk about diplomatic or military intervention we do clearly refer to a specific moment in time in which a state intervenes across boundaries of other states in such a way as to change their internal structure. If we talk about economic intervention, therefore, we should by analogy use the term only for a very small category of events, which, paradoxically, we would in practice more often term 'aid'; in other words, specific grants of money at a particular moment in time. Generally speaking, most of the economic influence of which the critics have been complaining, will turn out not to be of this character but instead forms part of the normal relationship between states and is as such fairly constant over a period of time. Intervention will, therefore, be treated here as a specific act designed to alter the balance between government and opposition in another state.

DIPLOMATIC INTERVENTION

Diplomatic intervention is the use of diplomatic personnel or other agents to assist or to prevent specific political changes in a foreign state.

Assuming that the two states have regular diplomatic relations, and that one of them is threatened by a revolutionary outbreak, the other may, on receiving reports of the outbreak, decide to extend an offer of support to the incumbent government. This may well alter the internal balance between government and opposition, but it is legitimate in international law and does not constitute intervention.

If, on the other hand, the decision is made to empower the accredited envoys to enter into relations with the opposition, even if these relations go no further than an exchange of views, this may be regarded as intervention by the government and the offending envoys declared *persona non grata*. For such purposes, therefore, governments make use in general of unofficial agents whose official character can if necessary be disavowed. A delicate situation then arises if, either by information privately received, or through an analysis of press reports and other public sources of information, the foreign power comes to believe either that its interests will be best served if the government agrees to talk to the opposition or else advises specific concessions. In such circumstances even an offer of mediation may be regarded as improper diplomatic intervention.

Mediation is a recognised diplomatic activity which consists simply in conveying the views of two parties to one another in such a way as to further agreement between them. For a foreign power to mediate in a revolutionary situation its mediation must first of all be acceptable to both sides, and this is by definition comparatively rarely the case. It may in the first instance therefore be necessary to involve another power in the chain of negotiation. The risk with this, however, is that the contending parties may then come to believe that the other two powers are acting in concert to secure their own ends.

In this connection a special role is attached to the United Nations, which has a specific duty to safeguard world peace. Though offers of mediation by the Secretary General may often be publicly resented by governments who see them as 'official' recognition of a state of belligerency they themselves would prefer to ignore or conceal, in practice they are more readily accepted among Third World states than the mediation of major powers. On the other hand, if the parties are to accept an agreement, they must believe that they are unlikely to get better terms, and it is at this point that unofficial representations from their major allies are of crucial importance.

Technically speaking, advice from another government that it considers the government likely to lose if it does not make concessions is not intervention. A statement to the effect that, if it does not concede, that government will forfeit its support, on the other hand, technically is intervention, and thus the United States Ambassador in Guatemala in 1954 intervened when he advised General Díaz, successor to President Arbenz, that he would not obtain the support of the United States. The withdrawal of envoys and the severance of diplomatic relations can follow as a public sign of withdrawal of support, as in the case of the Organisation of American States in 1979 at the time of the fall of President Anastasio Somoza Debayle. On that occasion the Government of Costa Rica took the even more controversial step of publicly permitting the formation of a Revolutionary Government on its soil and according it official recognition before Somoza had actually resigned. Under international law such an action could constitute grounds for a declaration of war, for it constitutes public and open aid to an opposition movement, but by that time the Somoza government was no longer able to respond in such a fashion. Normally, aid afforded to an insurgent movement is clandestine, and channelled through unofficial agents. It can take the form of passively permitting a revolutionary movement to raise funds, organise and prepare for combat on a neighbouring state, or of actively fomenting a revolutionary movement, in which case support for that movement may well take the form of armed menaces or actual military intervention.

To begin with, it will be recalled that insurgents have no standing in international law unless they are recognised as belligerents. But access to foreign governments is generally considered desirable by revolutionary movements to buy weapons and to secure diplomatic neutrality or even aid, and hence they will run considerable risks to make such contacts. A classic case was the two Confederate agents named Mason and Slidell who were travelling to Britain on a British vessel during the American Civil War when they were intercepted and taken off by a United States warship. On this occasion the Government of the United Kingdom protested at the interference with a British vessel and secured their release, but as unofficial agents they had no protection in their own right. There was, therefore, no reason in international law why such agents should not be captured, if in fact it is legitimate to do so. In fact it is quite clear that there are good grounds for a government insisting that other powers do not receive such agents, still less accede to their requests.

Here the classic instance is that of the Confederate agents who bought and fitted out the battleship *Alabama* in Liverpool. The *Alabama* was permitted to sail by the British government; that is, the British government failed to prevent it from sailing, and subsequently, through arbitration, was held guilty of negligence and had to pay an indemnity of £15m. The cancelled cheque for this amount was framed and hung over the Foreign Secretary's desk where it can still be seen as a reminder to succeeding foreign secretaries not to do it again! So the responsibility, therefore, of a state towards an established government of another power is firstly, *not* to receive the agents and secondly *not* to accede to their demands, particularly where they refer to the supply of arms. So any government receiving agents and any government, still more, permitting them to bear arms, is likely to get itself into trouble.

Despite this, the process is in fact highly institutionalised.

In the Chilean Civil War of 1891 the Congressional Party (which eventually won) sent agents both to Europe and to the United States for funds and to buy arms. It is not known, in this particular case, whether there were in fact regular agents in the United Kingdom through which they dealt. But there is no doubt that they dealt with regular agents in the United States, namely the law firm of Hopkins and Hopkins, who were lobbyists of the State Department in Congress. Anyone promoting a revolution in Latin America during the years 1891 to 1920 sent a representative to Hopkins and Hopkins in Washington, who proceeded to intercede with the State Department for them and lobby Congress quite legally and through the usual processes of American government. During the various revolutions in Mexico the provisional government (so-called) was represented in Washington. Madero's movement was represented by the so-called Vice-President of the provisional government, Francisco Vásquez Gómez. That of Carranza appointed José Vasconcelos, who later became one of the best-known of modern Mexican writers, and left his impressions of this time in his memoirs, which are very lively. At the same time a great many other agents operated on behalf of other movements in the small states and found themselves dealing through the same firm. It is most interesting to reflect on what would have happened if Hopkins and Hopkins had been briefed by both sides in the same dispute —in fact, they may well have been.

Since the 1920s, however, there has developed a different kind of situation. Before 1920, if a movement wanted help then it approached the nearest great power in its area and tried to get it to change its mind. Since it has been possible to play off two or more great powers against each other, in such a way as to maximise the advantages from each— one gets movements like, for example, the Bangladesh secessionists who succeeded in getting themselves made *persona grata* to absolutely everybody, so that they received aid from the United States on the one hand, and their leaders go for medical treatment to the Soviet Union on the other. The local arena, therefore, has been expanded into a world-wide one, and the role of the dominant power has been complicated by the intrusion of other powers.

It is, however, rather doubtful whether foreign aid is frequently an important factor. First of all, no coups, and very few revolutionary movements construed in the broadest possible sense, continue long enough to involve foreign intervention—diplomatic or otherwise (Rosenau 1964, p. 19). Secondly, the recognition of new governments today, therefore, tends to be primarily a question of recognising *faits accomplis*. In this situation unofficial agents do not appear to perform much of a role, and recommendations for recognition are made by regular diplomatic personnel, who would otherwise be out of a job.

Unofficial agents are also used by governments, where a government finds itself confronted with an insurgent movement in a country with which it feels, for the safety of its nationals and otherwise, it needs to deal. This is perfectly legitimate in terms of international law—but only if the agents are unofficial and engage only in discussion. Agreement with insurgent parties cannot be binding because they have no standing in international law. In rare cases governments send unofficial agents to insurgents in their own country; in other words, they open negotiations with an existing revolutionary movement in order to establish some kind of peace. This, however, is very seldom and only normally happens when the incumbent government has been defeated and wishes to yield gracefully. In practice, we are concerned rather more often with the sending of unofficial agents from governments to foreign insurgent movements which, as noted above, is a dangerous thing to do, as it is liable to be misconstrued.

It is hard to distinguish here between the three major categories of individuals operating in this situation. First of all, it can be assumed that most great powers were interested in the insurgent movement in the neighbouring country and will ensure that they have on the scene spies or *informants*, agents whose job it is to simply find out what is going on. The problem of sending such agents is that they tend to become committed to one or other side and to start actually trying to influence the situation, such as by establishing unofficial contact with a view to ultimate recognition.

If they do this, they move into the second category, that of *unofficial diplomatist*. Unofficial diplomatists are those that engage in diplomacy without having official status. This is most frequently, in practice, carried out by regular members of the diplomatic, or possibly the consular, corps; as for example, in the case of Sir Robert Bruce Lockhart who, as Consul, was in Moscow in 1917–18 and therefore was in the right place at the right moment when in fact the diplomats were still in Petrograd, and too far away to be able to tell what was going on. In such a case an agent on the spot may be empowered to engage in negotiations which otherwise would not come within his sphere of competence. Alternatively, one also gets people who are sent, or indeed who assume an unofficial diplomatic mission. This is particularly true in the case of Americans who have always been given to writing letters of good advice to their presidents, and if they happen to find themselves in the right place at the right moment, start trying to engage in a spot of unofficial diplomacy on their own account.

Occasionally there may be a third category of unofficial agents sent to a foreign country, the *agents provocateurs*, who try to cause trouble for a government which is considered to be dangerous or hostile, either by inciting an existing revolutionary movement or by attempting to stir up a revolutionary movement that is not yet in being.

Now it can be said that some kind of penetration by one or other of these means is probably almost impossible for a state to prevent. The days of slow communications and relatively sealed frontiers are now at an end. People can move with great speed, and large categories of people, such as tourists, relief personnel, communications personnel, are now in continual transit in almost all the countries of the world. It is no longer as easy to seal a frontier and to keep things under wraps as it once was. Even the People's Republic of China is now seeking to increase its tourist trade, while East Germany, which imposes strict limits on the movement of its citizens, is unable to prevent them from receiving West German broadcasts and even television programmes. It is therefore a relatively easy matter today to introduce a foreign agent into a hostile country and to maintain communications with him, though it is unlikely that, given the existence of a reasonably competent police force, that agent can engage in very high-level activities.

Outside all but the most developed countries, however, the government is not in effective control of a great deal of its national territory and things are very different. It is in such areas that opportunities arise which mean that the great powers no longer necessarily have to engage in overt military intervention in order to achieve their objectives. In the uncertain twilight zone between diplomatic activity and subversion there are numerous possibilities for a government that is not too scrupulous about the means it uses to secure its ends.

K. J. Holsti (1967) claims that in the period 1900–50, in 200 revolutions, intervention occurred in half that number and more than one intervention in a quarter. While it is undoubtedly true that multiple interventions are common, and not simply a product of the period of the Cold War, some caution is needed about these figures. Taking the narrower criterion of aid actually afforded during the active period of the revolutionary incident, the author found that in 364 incidents between 1901–60 aid was afforded to the government in 24 instances and to the opposition in 76 (Calvert 1970b, p. 219). Subsequent research has shown, however, that aid of this kind appears to be particularly significant in the population of successful incidents (Brier and Calvert, 1975; Brier 1982). Above all, it was strongly correlated with proximity to one or other of the superpowers, a fact that speaks for itself! Holsti concludes:

As a means of achieving objectives, defending interests or promoting social values abroad, governments may, instead of sending diplomatic notes or making military threats, infiltrate foreign voluntary organisations, sponsor strikes and riots, create political scandals, attempt a *coup d'état*, or, on their own territory, organise, train and arm a group of foreign dissidents and then send them home to conduct guerrilla warfare or subversion.

MILITARY INTERVENTION

The role of military intervention itself, however, is still a rather obscure one; for two reasons. To begin with the use of foreign intervention is often not practicable. Intervention, for example, of the United States in the Dominican Republic in 1965, where a very large amount of force could be brought to bear by a very large country on a relatively small situation, was feasible. So too was the Soviet intervention in Czechoslovakia in 1968. But it is not to be deduced from this that the United States government, for example, could land troops in Chile or Brazil, or the Soviet government, in France or Britain. Secondly, it is only realistic to say that the capacity to intervene indirectly is limited. Any attempt to use an overt military threat, for example, in the case of the Soviet Union to influence a change of government in Turkey, or in the case of the United States in Venezuela, one of the medium rank powers would probably create such a backlash of hostility, both in the country concerned and in the neighbouring countries, that it would be totally counter-productive.

The military threat, therefore, has been very much downgraded since 1945, in favour of unofficial guerrilla warfare, or similar action. There is no doubt that a considerable number of insurgent movements in being at any given moment receive a good deal of foreign support. Whether these come into the category of intervention or aid is a nice question. As they are in fact constant, it is probably difficult to describe them accurately as intervention, even today. The last of Holsti's categories, the organisation, training and arming of a group of foreign dissidents and sending them home to conduct guerrilla warfare or subversion certainly is intervention. American examples are the Bay of Pigs expedition to Cuba (1961) and the 'contras' in Honduras; a Soviet example is the training, through the North Korean training agency, of the various guerrilla agents who have been sent to Central America. Lesser powers can find such methods both convenient and cheap, as witness the late President Nkrumah's training ground in Ghana for freedom fighters to liberate the African continent, because this too had a certain limited role at this particular period of history.

It is true that we know most about the activities of the great powers, and we are inclined nowadays to pin the label of intervention specifically on the great powers. But caution is needed here. All types of powers practise clandestine activities, though not necessarily subversion. But it is not so easy to avoid the challenge of subversion—it is a very flexible concept. All countries like to be liked by their neighbours and if those neighbours involve, or have within their national boundaries, substantial minority groups who appeal to their fellows to join them, then this comes very definitely within the category of subversion. For example, the appeal to the Northern Irish of those of their compatriots who press their views, that they should become part of a unified Ireland, is one that, if it came from a great power to a little one, would be regarded as being subversion. In the case of a little power to a great power it is not traditional to regard it as subversion, and yet it is in fact indistinguishable. And the same kind of comment applies to a vast number of other situations, and also to situations in which the powers are reasonably equal in size.

The limitations on the nature of subversive appeals to neighbouring countries are fairly easily delineated. Firstly, there is the fortunate *scarcity of target groups*. Owing to the period after the First World War, in which people endeavoured as far as possible to redraw the map of the world, to keep international minorities at a minimum as far as possible, there are relatively few significant national minorities in countries other than Africa, where the boundaries, being both colonial and artificial, are still unforged. The target groups need to be of a certain size before they can actually or potentially prove to be a danger to a neighbouring state or limit its potential for action; if they are very small indeed, they may be a running sore to some government but they are not likely to be of very great significance. In fact, it is interesting to see how in the case of a country the size of Britain the action in Northern Ireland can in fact be contained and can be regarded as being of relatively small significance in terms of overall national politics. Even in a close election like the General Election of February 1974, Northern Ireland was only marginally significant, which is very interesting.

The *apathy of the target group* is the second limitation. Every so often enthusiastic zealots in Wales blow up water pipe lines, or South Tyroleans attack targets in Northern Italy to prove that they are really an Austrian minority. But the apathetic response of the majority of the populations of these areas suggests that they are not actively interested, as long as their governments treat them with moderate fairness.

Poor communications are a third factor. In many parts of the world national minorities are so concerned with staying alive and so far from any of the centres of population concentration, that their insurgency has little effect. An example are the Nagas in India. The Nagas are, of course, a revolutionary movement, and not the product of external subversion, but in fact Nagaland is so small and so peripheral as far as India is concerned that the conflict has been almost completely contained, while the neighbouring states are too remote to assist them.

Lastly, there is the *weakness of the claimant states*. Many states that in fact affect their neighbours through their appeals to shared minorities are not themselves very strong. Tunisia and Algeria function in this respect in Morocco. Morocco does the same for Mauretania and the Spanish Sahara; Ghana does for Nigeria and Togo for the Ivory Coast and Niger; Egypt for Yemen, South Yemen and Israel (Zartman 1966). Extend this pattern throughout the world and consider in fact just how many states have been medium-size irritants to their neighbours, without necessarily being able to secure a decisive shift of power in their favour.

Such problems are the stuff of international relations. Here we are interested in the revolutionary dimension, the possibility of stirring up informal dissension or appeal to minorities as a means to secure state objectives. Holsti (1967) identifies five specific factors determining the outcome of intervention in modern conditions.

Firstly—and it would be natural for an American to stress this first perhaps—we live in an age in which it is more or less universally accepted that great powers have a certain obligation towards the welfare of smaller ones. There are, therefore, programmes of economic and military aid in being all the time, in most parts of the world, which implies a degree of political interest in how those funds are spent. States accepting foreign aid *necessarily* accept a degree of derogation from their national sovereignty, if there can indeed still be said to be such a thing.

Secondly, it is a fact that in many of the extreme cases of actual military intervention, the intervention is in fact requested. In other words, where there is a great power with sufficient capacity to be called into play in an internal situation, then it is quite easy for it, as with the Soviet Union in Afghanistan, to arrange to be called in to intervene on behalf of the incumbent. And this is—given the present nature of international law—a perfectly legitimate action.

Thirdly, ideological affiliations transcend state boundaries. We do not live only in the era of the national minority, we also live in an era of political strife. Such ideas create common interests across boundaries. Fourthly, many governments today come to power through the use of force and therefore they quite naturally tend to use force in securing their further objectives. Having used force to gain power, they use it to secure any other objectives which they may have in mind. (See Calvert 1976.)

And last, but not least, there is the nuclear stalemate. The existence of the nuclear stalemate predisposes countries to seek a balance of advantage within the international system by use of subversion or otherwise (cf. Herz 1959).

We can therefore, to sum up, identify six levels of intervention. First of all there is the level of *diplomatic intervention* in the internal affairs of a state—where a country deliberately uses diplomatic weight in order to try to secure a governmental outcome which is favourable to it. An example which is frequently cited is that of the United States ambassador in Greece, Ambassador Puerifoy in 1952. But this is a poor example for many reasons because Greece fell clearly, according to the famous terms of the bargain at Yalta between Churchill and Roosevelt, on the one hand, and Stalin on the other, within the Western sphere of influence and therefore was recognised as such. What we tend to forget, however, is that there are other examples which were much less happy than this. For example, at the end of the war the incumbent American ambassador in Argentina, Spruille Braden, took a dislike to Perón and arranged the publication of a blue book on national subversion in Latin America during the war, in which it was made quite clear that Perón was regarded in Washington as pro-Nazi. Then all the *Peronistas* had to do was campaign on the slogan 'Perón or Braden' and the result was, of course needless to say, a landslide for Perón.

The State Department very nearly repeated the same mistake in the case of Vargas in Brazil. They were strongly urged by their resident ambassador in Rio to issue a public statement calling for the democratisation of Brazil at the end of the war, and they actually issued such a statement and then hurriedly realised that it was going to produce almost exactly the opposite effect to the one they intended, so they very sensibly did not continue with it and the result was in fact, before the election itself, the institution of a civilian republican government. So diplomatic experience, in other words, as I have stressed, makes uncertain precedent. It is undoubtedly the lowest level of intervention and one which is commonplace *in favour of* an existing government. It is relatively rare to use diplomatic intervention *against* an incumbent government if only because it is not likely to work.

Then it is possible to use *clandestine political action*, that is, where a power may make use of allegedly internal actions in order to try and overturn an incumbent government, actions such as bribery, the planting of rumours or stories and sending of anonymous letters, and even, on rare occasions, political assassination. All these examples are rather unusual. Because the United States is, in fact, an indigenous base for them, it is not likely that they will receive a great deal of support there, for other than for ideological reasons, and in an age in which ideological considerations are paramount, the ideological net is spread rather wide. In other words, since the contending great powers have succeeded in getting a great many minorities sympathetic to themselves in many different countries, it means that effort is in fact spread extremely thin.

Thirdly, a state may use *demonstrations of force*. The Lebanon landings in 1958 were not merely an attempt by the United States to forestall the communisation of the Lebanon itself, they were also intended to serve notice on the Soviet Union that any attempt to intervene in the internal affairs of Lebanon by subversion or otherwise would be resisted by the United States, and by derivation, to strengthen the position of the United States generally in the Middle East. The deployment of a US fleet off the Dominican Republic in 1961 was made for a different reason, to serve notice on the surviving members of the Trujillo family that the United States required their removal from Dominican politics. This they did, but not before one of them had personally machine-gunned to death the men responsible for the assassination of his late father, the former president of the country (Diederich 1978).

Subversion may be used to make a country less capable of resisting an internal as well as an external attack. The Nazi putsch in Czechoslovakia in 1938 found key Nazi sympathisers in all key positions, as did the Soviet putsch in 1948 find communists already installed where they could ensure that the takeover went without interruption. The activities of the American CIA in Iran in 1952 in creating the climate for the fall of Mossadegh and the return to power of the Shah would also fall into this category (Wise and Ross 1964).

Subversion does not necessarily imply the existence of a state of unconventional warfare, although it may well act either as a prelude or as an accompaniment to it. Nor should it be assumed that all such occurrences are subversive in origin. Following the Cuban Revolution in 1959, a number of guerrilla movements, as we have seen, appeared in imitation of the Cubans, notably in Colombia, Venezuela, Guatemala and Peru (Gott 1970; cf. Debray 1969). The only campaign that developed out of an expedition planned and outfitted from Cuba for the purpose, however, was the unsuccessful expedition of Che Guevara to Bolivia in 1966–7. On the other hand, a power with sufficient resources to spare may achieve much more considerable results by actively extending aid to indigenous movements, such as that of the Sandinistas in Nicaragua, who received aid from Costa Rica, Panama and Cuba. The United States has since charged that the FMLN in El Salvador is receiving aid from Cuba via Nicaragua; in return they have aided the counter-revolutionary forces in Honduras which have been striking down into northern Nicaragua (McMichael and Paulus 1983, Stamford Central American Action Network, 1983).

Lastly, as we have seen, a power may choose to intervene militarily with its own forces in a revolutionary situation, though the risks of doing so are considerable and the rewards of success unlikely to justify the risks.

9. Counter-insurgency

Counter-insurgency, for the purposes of this discussion, will in the first instance be taken as a neutral term referring to the various techniques and theories that relate to the prevention of insurgencies, and an *insurgency* as some kind of uprising against an incumbent government. In fact, in sociology, insurgency has been used much more generally to define a phenomenon within any kind of organisation which is characterised by dissension over the way in which the organisation is being directed. In the political sense, however, we normally mean by insurgency a form of armed insurrection. Hence, most of the people who are interested in counter-insurgency are military strategists, and agents of incumbent governments, one of whose duties it is to maintain some sort of strategic order. It has, therefore, over the past thirty years, come to mean a form of strategy which is mainly military and within the military context, one designed to fight irregular, especially guerrilla, war.

For any such military action to succeed there are, however, two preconditions that are so obvious that their importance is often neglected. Most people in most countries believe that the best chance of avoiding insurgency altogether lies in having good government; but then people differ considerably on what they class as a good government. Secondly, it is generally agreed by experts that effective counter-insurgency must involve political action by civilians as well as military action by soldiers. In fact there is in counter-insurgency no easy distinguishing line between the two. Soldiers have to operate in a political context and civilians for their own safety have to operate in a military one, and as a result of this a good deal of confusion has grown up.

For there is in fact a very wide range of political situations in which insurgency occurs, or may occur, depending on the nature of the arena chosen (urban or rural) and the status of the territory in which it occurs (a province, a dependent territory, a protectorate or a friendly state), as well as on the political order of the state that is combating the insurgency (liberal democracy, authoritarian government or dictatorship).

The term counter-insurgency has come to be used since 1945 specifically to designate a struggle against rural move- ments in a colonial or quasi-colonial situation, and, not surprisingly, the views both of civilians and military advisers tend to be particularly strongly coloured by their most recent experiences. These influences are therefore predominantly reflected in the available literature. This literature, too, is the product of writers in liberal democratic states in which domestic public opinion has proved to be one of the major targets of insurgent action. Again, the literature reflects this. There are three main types: books on how insurgencies have been successfully countered, usually concentrating on the military aspects of the struggle, aimed at the general reader; books for specialists on the same subject; and books seeking to show that the first two categories are wrong. Of this last category, as we shall see, a consistent theme has been the debasement, as their authors see it, of the principles of the liberal democratic state when confronted with an armed insurgency, the most extreme form of which is the thesis that repeated or prolonged involvement in counter-insurgency creates what is termed alternatively the 'counter-insurgency state' or 'national security state', namely a state in which military necessity is used to make a government virtually independent of the political inputs which it nominally must depend upon for its authority, as, for example, in the case of the Nixon Administration and Vietnam.

Mention of the Nixon Administration, however, should alert us to the fact that this literature is very much the product of a period and of one country, the United States, where the particular tradition of American government led its chief foreign policymakers (Nixon and Kissinger) to carry to extremes the assumption that they might safely do any- thing that did not arouse too great a public outcry. This tendency was, as P. E. Haley has shown (Haley 1982), some- thing that had grown up over the post-1945 period as a work- ing assumption that had not previously been put to the test. Its failure was inevitable, given the structure of the American constitutional system, as soon as it was challenged by any substantial body of public opinion, and, in the event, the generation of such a body of public opinion was strongly encouraged by the feeling of deceit and betrayal that the 'politics of acquiescence' had hitherto not encountered.

The United States is, however, a most unusual country even by the standards of liberal democracies, and in the post-war period had only confronted insurgencies in the Philippines and Indo-China, before the advent of the Reagan Administration led to its increasing involvement in Central America. In the same period, there also occurred the campaigns of Portugal in Angola, Mozambique, Guiné and Cabo Verde; the Netherlands in Indonesia and Dutch New Guinea (Irian Barat); France in Indo-China, Tunisia, Morocco and Algeria; and the United Kingdom in Greece, Palestine, Kenya, Cyprus, Malaya, Borneo, South Yemen and Northern Ireland. So there are plenty of examples to go on, and it is specifically these sorts of examples that we need to compare with the United States experience. In the literature that has grown up around these examples emphasis is still on the military rather than the civilian combating of these insurgent movements. The only point of considerable difference between the countries is, of course, the economic resources available. The United States, despite all allegations to the contrary, had enormous resources compared with the other states mentioned and despite all mistakes which it made, which were numerous, was able to sustain a lengthy war in Vietnam (1965–75). This succeeded in achieving essentially what it set out to do, namely the countering of communist insurgency in the southern part of Vietnam. It did not succeed in conquering North Vietnam, nor did it even succeed in turning back the communists and North Vietnamese forces already entrenched in South Vietnam.

Britain, during the period 1946–67, was often very stretched. On the other hand, Portugal, a very small country in comparison, sustained an even longer campaign than that of the United States. This casts doubt on the theory that a very large force is proportionately necessary to counter insurgency by military means. The famous example generally given is that there were fifteen times as many British troops in Malaya as there were guerrillas. It took 6,500 hours for an individual soldier on patrol to even see one guerrilla, let alone actually shoot him. The belief therefore grew up that it is not possible to counter insurgency by military means alone, unless the balance of forces is quite disproportionate to the goals to be achieved.

This has been extended by certain left-wing writers into the theory that it is not possible to counter insurgency at all, but this is not quite true, as the examples of Palestine, Cyprus and Malaya make quite clear. It is possible; the question for government is, is one willing to take the consequences of doing so? If the government is not 'good' enough to avert insurgency altogether, it is probably true that the best chance of its suppressing an insurgent movement lies in that period of its development which corresponds to Mao's stages one and two; in other words, at the point at which the insurgency is moving from preparation to action; being transformed from being clandestine into being overt. The next best chance comes at the stage at which the rebels try to transform the guerrilla movement campaign or sporadic terrorist acts into a regular military movement committted to destroy government.

Curiously enough, Mao, on the one hand, and, for example, Sir Robert Thompson on the other, agree on this point; that the point of initial operations is that at which insurgencies are most vulnerable. Once an insurgent movement is already in being, and is larger than a certain size, the government will have to put up a very disproportionate amount of effort and stand a relatively small chance of being able to reduce it. Hence alertness to the possible emergence of such movements is crucial.

Another factor that is very important to remember is that just because the number of guerrillas in a rural peasant situation, or a number of urban terrorists, in a situation such as Cyprus or Northern Ireland, is very small, it does not mean that the government can ignore them. It is probable that the forces actually engaged on the part of the so-called Provisional IRA in Northern Ireland, have at most times been as low as 200, rather than the 2,000 which is always quoted in the British press. Then, by definition, it is extremely difficult to get rid of them completely, for as long as there is a small number of people left—too small to easily be caught, but too large to be negligible—then it is very difficult to persuade civilians that the movement is at an end. The government may well, therefore, have to take a risk, at a certain stage, as for example did the government in Malaya (1960), of simply declaring the insurgency to be at an end.

The first and most important lesson of counter-insurgency is the importance of maintaining the primacy of civilian government. A government confronted with a domestic emergency should make the minimum possible use of emergency powers, since resort to them gives the opposition a powerful propaganda card, by suggesting at least that the government is badly shaken and at worst that it is becoming dictatorial and ignoring the principles of justice. Thus the decision by the government of Mr Brian Faulkner to introduce internment in Northern Ireland can be seen to have destroyed the minimal political consensus that was required if a political settlement based on the integral unity of Northern Ireland was to be maintained. Since that time, direct rule from Westminster, for the Parliament at which the citizens of Northern Ireland at least have a vote, has been the only solution that in practice (though not in theory) has been accepted as the best available in the circumstances.

In the case of insurgency in a colonial territory, best results have been achieved where, as in Malaya, the colonial government has had the option open to it of handing over power in the medium term to an elected civilian government that can command popular support, and has been prepared to embrace this opportunity. Where, as with the Smith regime in Rhodesia, the need to accept such a transfer is accepted too late, the probability is that the more extreme factions in the insurgent movement will have gained so much ground that to all intents and purposes it will have succeeded in its original purpose.

In the case of an insurgency in a friendly state, however, the situation is very much more difficult. In South Vietnam and Cambodia, as earlier in South Korea, the United States found itself bound by the concept of its obligations to give military support to a government with only tenuous claims to constitutional origin or popular support. Vietnamese peasants subjected to military government rightly felt that a victory for that government would mean the surrender of the lands expropriated by them in the Delta region of the Mekong (Sansom 1970). There at least the concept of constitutionality had already virtually disappeared. In the case of Cambodia, however, the military coup that displaced Prince Sihanouk and established the short-lived Khmer Republic destroyed the only traditional authority that had been able to mediate between the army on the one hand and the communists on the other, supported by the force of nationalism which the Prince personified. The result was the disastrous power-vacuum when United States forces were withdrawn, which was filled by a highly radicalised Khmer Rouge bent on revenge and determined to eradicate all trace of its predecessors.

Counter-insurgency forces operating in a friendly state must always be liable to be regarded by the local inhabitants as anti-national, if not indeed as an occupying force. After all, British forces were so regarded by French peasants during the First World War, and United States forces similarly by the West Germans after 1950. The situation is then complicated by the possibility, already visible in El Salvador, that attempts to encourage the government to adopt more democratic practices will be used by the government itself as a pretext for nationalistic resistance, which its members often naively believe will bring them genuine political popularity. This is an extreme case. A government can simply disregard such pressure from its allies; it does not have to oppose it publicly unless it chooses, because it knows that its allies, once committed to battle, have little alternative in their own domestic environment but to accomplish their mission. Even if a civilian government does pay attention to the advice it is given, moreover, it is likely that, as in the Salvadorean case again, it will find that it is unable to count on the obedience of its own military commanders, to whom the fact of the insurgency makes it virtually subject.

The next important thing for a successful counter-insurgency campaign is to understand the mind of the opposition. It is here that the literature of counter-insurgency is most seriously deficient, and at worst highly tendentious, supporting an extreme right-wing interpretation of post-war events in which little or no room is left for the possibility that the rebels might have a point or two on their side (cf. Crozier 1960; Osanka 1962; Paret and Shy 1962, Thayer 1963; Pustay 1965; Taber 1965). The best accounts (e.g. Thompson 1970) of post-war insurgency therefore need the added corrective of studies by academic observers or other writers more detached from events, as with Anthony Short's excellent analysis of the Malayan Emergency (Short 1974). What is clear from all these and the other available sources is that specialists in counter-insurgency still conceive of counter-insurgency in military terms, with the inevitable corollary that success depends on certain kinds of military preconditions being met. Provided we remember that these are not the only conditions, and hence that their absence does not necessarily imply defeat for the incumbent government, we can note the principal points that emerge.

1. *Planning.* Planning is the most essential prerequisite of a successful counter-insurgency campaign and its absence has led to more serious trouble than any other omission. A government confronted for the first time with the threat of an armed insurgency tends to give a panic response. The immediate imposition of emergency regulations, and the dispatch of troops in an unprepared state, who, if heavily armed, are all too likely to loose off ammunition in all directions, is the first serious mistake in alienating a civilian population and driving recruits into the hands of the insurgents. The first response to an armed threat should be through the police and not the armed forces, and the very minimum additional force should be brought to bear on the situation so as to avoid the psychological consequences of an apparent defeat in a public confrontation. If armed forces are to be deployed, vital strategic links and communications must first be clearly established, and the aim of the intervention closely defined.

The essential links that are necessary are (as applicable) those between the army and the police, the army and other military forces, and between the government and the provincial authorities that may report incidents and require military support at short notice. All such action must be refused unless it fits in with the overall strategic plan. To do otherwise is to risk forces being pinned down in static defensive positions and the loss of the overall initiative. Alternatively, rivalry between the services, or between the services and the police, may grow to such an extent that effective combined operations become impossible. The key, therefore, is to maintain the supremacy of the civil power, to which military operations must remain subordinate. At national level this is achieved through a civilian 'war cabinet' and at provincial level through civilian and military commissioners working very closely with one another but with primacy always to the former.

2. *Intelligence*. Successful planning depends on good intelligence. At the outset of an insurgency, if the government has indeed been taken by surprise, intelligence is obviously deficient and will have to be rectified. Again, there is no substitute for careful preparation and the use of time to develop the necessary structures. As noted above, it will be the aim of the insurgent to deny all knowledge of his activities to the government, while obtaining the fullest knowledge of the government's activities, and it will be the objective of the government to reverse this state of affairs.

The insurgent, however, starts with the advantage of secrecy and surprise, and may well have made the disruption of intelligence networks by sabotage or diversion part of his original strategic plan. In the government's favour is its unique characteristic of legitimacy. It therefore has the 'right' to use force against the insurgent, whether the insurgent likes it or not, and enjoys in most cases a good deal of residual support from normal law-abiding citizens. The government's aim must therefore be to achieve total information about the insurgent and deny information about its own actions.

In practice this is relatively difficult since it is large and therefore its movements are evident. But it is also extremely rare, in fact, for insurgents to have a great deal of information. It is clear that in the anti-colonial struggles their local knowledge was limited as long as security was maintained and forces did not become overconfident. The only time that an urban terrorist movement has enjoyed the great knowledge theoretically possible to it was the Tupamaros movement in Uruguay, where it appears that the government and revolutionary personnel were more nearly identical than could be imagined, for the government elite was riddled with insurgent sympathisers (Labrousse 1970).

3. *Training*. It is obviously important to train counter-insurgency personnel in the appropriate techniques. Many of the techniques for which armies are normally trained, like using machine-guns or bazookas, firing artillery, driving tanks or exploding nuclear weapons, have the effect of blasting a whole street or neighbourhood out of existence. To do this seems perfectly normal in conventional war, but in counter-insurgency the effects on the government's public image of competence is fatal. Troops therefore have to be trained to special purposes, and the more so since governments have to make use of the recruits available. Many, as cannot too often be remembered, are dependent for their supply of other ranks (enlisted men) on conscription—Britain and the United States are among the few countries in the world relying on an all-volunteer army. Some senior officers and politicians have always liked the idea of conscription as it means a larger army. Conversely, it means less security. Raw troops can be trained more easily because they are raw, but they have to be renewed at frequent intervals just when they have achieved proficiency in the necessary skills. Thirdly, conscript troops bring with them an ever-present risk of disaffection. This is much less likely in a colonial situation but particularly dangerous in a domestic one, where the custom is to rotate troops from one province to another to avoid the fraternisation that may make them a particular risk.

Just as we have seen guerrillas in particular rely on a kind of 'militia' to relieve their scarce combat forces of unnecessary burdens, so too must the government establish such forces to relieve its cadres of specially-trained counter-insurgency forces. Needless to say, it is no less important that these militia forces be well trained. The nearer they can approximate to a police role rather than a military one, the better. The point that must be stressed is that this must be the case from the beginning of the campaign. If a government is unable to persuade its people to defend it, no amount of foreign troops are likely to be successful in doing so; the 'Vietnamisation' of the American presence in Indo-China came much too late, and indeed was a mere political excuse for the Nixon Administration to withdraw from an untenable position. Had the huge build-up of American forces in 1965 been resisted, and the aid begun under President Kennedy quietly extended, the subsequent history of events would have been very different. It is more than probable that a South Vietnamese government would still survive, and it is almost certain that if this had been the case, then Cambodia and Laos would still retain their previous neutralist governments.

4. *Technology*. Note has already been made of the disadvantages of technology as applied to the use of arms. This, however, is at least an old problem. Ever since the first caveman, whoever he was, found he could throw a rock at his neighbour and kill him without having to engage in hand-to-hand combat, governments have preferred to use technology rather than sacrificing men. The problem is that technology no longer does this; though the lives sacrificed are different lives, they are also more numerous and the effects more indiscriminate. Part of the reason, however, has less to do with arms as such than the general advance of technology in other fields. In Vietnam, for example, the Americans found that their aircraft actually flew too fast. This did not matter when approaching an industrial target that could be sighted and destroyed by radar; insurgents, however, were hard to detect without the use of the human eye. Special aircraft thus had to be built or adapted to act as 'spotters', like the Argentine *Pucará* during the period of the 'dirty war' (1976–9).

In the meantime, however, permanent problems were created for the campaign as a whole. Much wasted effort went into trying to pretend that people were not being hit more or less at random. Bombing of jungle trails was almost completely futile, but it terrified civilians. Defoliants poisoned them and blighted their crops, for which compensation, if offered, always came too late. Worst of all was napalm, used precisely because of its ability to destroy all life within range. The horror of seeing people who had been burned to death—or worse, badly burned but not dead— with napalm was so appalling that it destroyed confidence in any government that made use of it. Hence, in countering rural insurgency in Vietnam, the reliance on technology was strongly counterproductive.

On the other hand, there have been certain ways in which technology has helped governments rather than insurgents in towns. Towns are the natural habitat of governments, and it is very hard to challenge their use of authority successfully on their own terrain. The use of shield, helmets, water cannon, non-lethal gases, rubber or plastic 'bullets', trained sniffer dogs and bomb-disposal teams have enabled governments to meet the insurgent challenge in towns and to demonstrate their competence to do so, without killing their own citizens. The speeding-up of communications, of which governments have a monopoly, helps too, since it enables them to deploy their police and military forces much more quickly. Thus, a gathering crowd can be met with an effective counter-insurgency response before the enthusiasm of its members has reached the pitch of being prepared to take on a superior force with inadequate preparation. Again the ability to do so, however, depends always on the superior training of the forces involved, and casualties must always be avoided, even at the cost of casualties among the security forces, if the government is to retain its essential claim to legitimacy.

THE DOCTRINE OF COUNTER-INSURGENCY

The history of counter-insurgency in the twentieth century has shown a natural tendency to develop in parallel with developments in the concept of insurgency itself. In the first period after 1945 down to the mid-1960s, the main theatre of insurgency was the countryside. Accordingly, the literature reflects in this period an overwhelming concern with the guerrilla and how to fight him.

Guerrilla warfare, as a development of partisan warfare, was well understood to be dependent on an infrastructure of civilian support for motivation, the supply of food and other material resources, and the provision of disguise. In the very special circumstances of multi-racial Malaya, physical separation in the form of a resettlement programme was highly effective in cutting off the supply of food and making effective disguise almost impossible. What made it relatively easy to achieve, however, was the fact that in the divided community, the majority had a strong reason to accept it, and the creation of the so-called 'white areas' gave a practical demonstration of the effectiveness of the technique.

In Malaya, therefore, psychological warfare was aimed primarily at the small number of active terrorists, with the aim of encouraging them to surrender. The combined effects of isolation, fear and hunger led many to do so, once they knew that they could do so in safety. As far as the civilian population were concerned, the most effective psychological stimulus was the truth; that the country was moving steadily towards independence under a multi-racial government and that the number of insurgents, never great, was steadily declining.

In Algeria, on the other hand, the French found themselves in a very different position. A small minority in the Muslim majority, the French were not willing to move towards independence and were confronted with a substantial difficulty in maintaining their support among the civilian population as neighbouring states moved towards, and eventually achieved, independence. In the first instance they had borrowed from their wartime experience the notion of *la guerre psychologique* (psychological warfare) in the style of Chakotin, involving large-scale propaganda in 1930s style. With this precedent in Indo-China, United States forces used loud hailers, leaflets, radio broadcasts and comics, and indeed anything that seemed to serve the purpose, to put over the message that they were helping to defend freedom in Vietnam, and drive a wedge between the civilians and the guerrillas. As already noted, however, the overpowering effect of their tactics and firepower destroyed the goodwill that they were at such pains to create, and the massacre at My Lai was only the culmination of this process of alienation, much of which was both unintentional and unintended (Miller and Aya 1971). The creation of 'strategic hamlets' did not succeed in driving a wedge between the guerrillas and their supporters because the two could not be distinguished. Instead, it offered a series of hostages to fortune and facilitated the selective assassination of rural political leaders who were willing to take orders from the government.

Faced with such pressure and such uncertainties, it appears that the Americans did at times, as the French had before them, succumb to the temptation to employ what the French had earlier euphemistically, but entirely misleadingly, termed '*l'action psychologique*', more properly termed counter-terror. No army can ever be immune from the temptation to use counter-terror, particularly after a particularly bloody terrorist attack launched with all the advantages of surprise and rejection of the customary usages of regular warfare. But it has repeatedly been demonstrated to be a disastrous course if not checked. It is natural for guerrillas to believe that they will be tortured and killed if they fall into the hands of the government. It is understandable if terrorists caught in the act of planting bombs and suchlike are manhandled by police or security forces, and there is much evidence from conventional war that prisoners are quite frequently shot to avoid the trouble of bringing them in. But the large-scale use of force to try to coerce a civilian population into accepting an unpopular government or regime is bound to confirm the certainty that both these things will happen, and so do exactly what its proponents seek to avoid, create a bond between active insurgents and civilians.

It was the objective of creating a school of counter-insurgency methods that President John F. Kennedy set himself when he came to power, and there can be no doubt that in the early 1960s, especially in Latin America, its trainees were highly successful. As W. W. Rostow put it in a speech at Fort Bragg in 1961: 'My point is that we are up against a form of warfare which is powerful and effective only when we do not put our minds clearly to work on how to deal with it.' (Osanka 1962.) With the additional advantage of such training, the Bolivian army proved easily capable of rounding up Che Guevara's expedition in 1967; his subsequent death was, however, the most dramatic evidence, if that were needed, that the successful forces did not know when to stop.

In the second stage, after 1967, counter-insurgency was to evolve into the 'justification' for what was later known as the 'national security state' in the 1970s and 1980s. The 'national security state' was typically a Latin American military government obsessed with the overall objective of permanently eliminating foreign 'subversion' by the imprisonment, torture and execution of political opponents, many of whom had no connection with any form of insurgent activity. Fuelled by inter-service rivalry, such military establishments built up vast 'intelligence' organisations whose functions had little enough to do with real intelligence—the gathering and evaluation of information. These were in fact secret police under another name. Both Argentina and Brazil in the late 1960s, Guatemala after 1967, and Chile and Uruguay after 1973, evolved into 'national security states', and in Argentina and Brazil heads of 'intelligence' organisations were to be found even in the Presidency of the Republic.

Several factors were responsible for this change. To begin with, the number of trained personnel, always small, was swallowed up in the indigenous tradition of military government and repression, and their training dissipated. Secondly, the arena of conflict had, after the kidnapping of US Ambassador Gordon Mein in Guatemala in 1967, visibly shifted away from the countryside to the big cities where the majority of the population of Latin Americans lived. The student revolt in Europe and North America had its counterparts there, and, as with the Tupamaros, the unpredictable and spontaneous nature of what were often foolhardy gestures on their part aroused unreasoning primitive panic in police and soldiers, who responded by firing on crowds and rounding up suspects wholesale. In the mid-1970s many of these suspects then simply 'disappeared', as in Chile, or were 'transferred', in Argentina—in both cases, to hastily-dug graves or to the sea, or, to demonstrate their point, as has since become commonplace in Guatemala and El Salvador, to refuse tips and gullies.

The developed powers of Europe and North America found very soon that the threats with which they too appeared to be confronted were in fact very easily tackled, though not without some minor risks. It was an irony that the development of the 'national security state' coincided with the growth of expertise in the technology and practice of countering urban terrorism which proved more than adequate to achieve its purpose without the use of counter-terror (cf. Oppenheimer 1970).

Basic to the maintenance of urban control was the existence of well-trained police forces. Equipped with modern weapons and gadgetry, such forces proved easily able to counter mass demonstrations. Speedy, radio-equipped cars and even helicopters enabled them to deploy with great success against individual terrorists, and improved methods both of bomb disposal and of forensic investigation enabled them to check the impact of urban terrorism and to run to earth at least some of its users without having to resort to methods endangering civilians to any additional extent (Clutterbuck 1973).

Two new uses for political violence that at first appeared even more alarming to government and the general public also responded to careful and considered responses in which violence was at best wholly avoided and at worst kept to the very minimum. These were the kidnapping of ambassadors and other distinguished figures and the hijacking of aircraft.

Kidnapping was designed to secure a number of aims; to raise money through ransom, to destroy the credibility of governments that 'failed' to 'prevent' it, and to secure the release of prisoners both to strengthen the cause and to demonstrate their ability to safeguard their members. It was best countered by a firm refusal to make concessions. This procedure obviously had its risks for the hostages, the taking of whom western governments, notably West Germany, found it difficult to tolerate, but once the procedure was used, the government in question was rarely troubled the same way again. Brazil, on the other hand, which did make concessions, found that further demands followed.

Hijacking was even more embarrassing, since the hostages, being civilians, could not be regarded as having consented to the risks of their position. The introduction of metal detectors at airports and the agreement of governments not to receive hijackers under the International Convention on Air Piracy (1971) proved, however, in the end to be highly effective.

The worst casualties of this period occurred where international rather than internal conflict was the prime cause.
The death of the Israeli athletes at Munich resulted from
faulty police technique, as did the disastrous aftermath of the
abortive Egyptian attempt to prove at Larnaca airport,
Cyprus, that they could be as effective in a lightning counter-
strike against a terrorist hijacking as the Israelis themselves
had been at Entebbe airport, Uganda. Even in the latter the
effect of the strike was somewhat spoilt by the murder in
hospital of the only hostage not freed, Mrs Dora Bloch, who
was killed, moreover, not by the terrorists, but by the forces
of General Amin that were supposed to be protecting her.

In fact, the very range and effectiveness of the responses
of Western governments to these two apparently very new
and threatening developments are the surest sign that the
development of the 'national security state' was, in terms of
its ostensible purpose, quite unnecessary. It was to disappear
again slowly after 1979, as the internal contradiction of
military rule in developing countries began to become too
great to be managed, but not before it had cast guilt by
association on the governments not only of the United
States, but of lesser powers such as the United Kingdom
which had sold the 'national security states' arms and
extended to them credits which they used in the control of
their own citizens. Moreover, two of these states, Somoza's
Nicaragua and Shah Reza Pahlevi's Iran, succumbed to the
very revolutions that the elaborate structure of secret police
and repressive forces was designed to avert.

It is a matter for particular regret that the initiative that
did most to offset these harmful associations for the United
States, President Carter's stand on human rights, was not
only abandoned by the incoming Reagan Administration,
but explicitly reversed. It is hard to think of any more serious
blunder that they might have perpetrated. To reverse such
a policy, once adopted, was not by any means the same thing
as failing to adopt it in the first place. Hence, in this respect
at least, the Reagan Administration will be regarded as much
more at fault than the Nixon Administration or its predecessors.

THE CAMELOT PROBLEM

The sensitivity of governments to any hint of subversion has brought awkward consequences for the social scientist. To conclude, therefore, it will be useful to take a look at the fate of Project Camelot, which illustrates some of these problems.

Camelot, the legendary site of King Arthur's capital, was the private name used by the Kennedys to describe the Presidency of John F. Kennedy. Project Camelot, however, was the brainchild of the US army's Special Operations Research Organization (SORO) in 1964, and was described as 'a study whose objective is to determine the feasibility of developing a general social systems model which would make it possible to predict and influence politically significant aspects of social change in the developing nations of the world' (Horowitz 1967). In other words, it was an attempt to develop a mathematical model to predict revolution and to show how it could be averted. Funded by the US Department of Defence to the tune of $1–1½ million a year for three to four years, it would have been by far the biggest social science research project known up to that time.

Social scientists are quite rightly jealous of their right to research into any aspect of society they like, and the participants in the project gave a number of reasons why they were prepared to take part. Some held that money was needed for 'big social science' and that this was a legitimate way to secure it, with freedom of investigation guaranteed by the RAND Corporation. Some argued that the army had to be educated if mankind were to avert nuclear holocaust and make the world a better place to live in. None of them considered that they would be engaging in spying or other improper activities, and indeed in so far as the product of the research might be to uphold the existing government of a country against an insurgent challenge there was no legal objection in international law to them finding out what they would. What there was, of course, was a reasonable doubt as to whether the applied side of the project, if it involved the use of the US army, might involve inadmissible intervention, and it was this connection that created great alarm in Latin America, where the first news of the project leaked out in May 1965, unfortunately almost coincident with the American intervention in the Dominican Republic.

The existence of the project was disclosed by a visiting US academic to the rector of a Chilean university, whose allegations of spying achieved wide publicity in the press. In turn, the US Ambassador complained to the State Department, who in turn complained to the President that Defence were interfering in their province. In the end Defence cancelled the project, to save SORO and other social science projects that it already had elsewhere.

The project seems to have been no great loss to knowledge. The evidence is that its research design was both faulty and hopelessly over-ambitious, and as a result it was unlikely to have contributed much to our knowledge of revolution. As for the allegations of spying, that is a difficult problem. Research into the causes of revolution as such is certainly not spying. There will always be complaints from the left that its findings may be used to prevent revolution and from the right that they may be used to promote it, but as revolution is a process of interaction between government and opposition, both are right and both are wrong. Certainly, to secure the necessary degree of impartiality it is clearly crucial that the sources of funding should be academically impartial and free from direct control by the agency of any government. It may well be difficult to secure such funding, as such agencies tend to like 'safe' projects on everyday problems of society near at home. But it is not impossible.

10. Conclusion

There is no great mystery about revolution. It is not an immense driving force, a 'locomotive' of history, and the basis for understanding it is to be found, not in the realms of speculation about the human condition, but in the day-to-day world of power politics and coalition-building. It is, quite simply, the politics of violence.

The purpose of this book was to explore the nature of revolution in the context of international politics, and, by doing so, to cast new light on the nature of international politics today. What the student of international relations needs above all is to be able to assess the probability of any given kind of upheaval or socio-political change in a given area, and, next to that, to have a better idea of how to react to such changes when they occur. This investigation has shown how difficult it is to reach down into the human mind and to try to say which leaders will arise and what sort of support they will gather, but it also makes clear that once leaders and their movements have actually emerged, understanding what is likely to happen next can be at the least immensely helped, not only by possessing a record of information about how such movements and events have proceeded in the past, but in relating all such information by use of a comprehensive general theory. This is the task of social science. What then are the principal conclusions we can draw from this investigation?

We can see more clearly, to start with, how revolution has come to be seen as a politically desirable aspiration, and why its would-be practitioners have been so reluctant to accept the lessons of the past. In conjunction with others they hope to escape from the restraints of 'normal' politics, and to act politically without having at the same time to accept political restraints. Revolutionary politics is, however, normal politics in an unusual situation, as revolutionary leaders are leaders first and revolutionaries afterwards. To break the working rules under which the political system operates is a strategy which no referee exists to decree inadmissible. But it has its risks, the chief one of which seems to be the strong tendency for the socio-political order to return to its traditional style of operation, trapping the revolutionaries in the process of change that they have helped to set in motion.

We can see, secondly, why, although revolutionaries are many, revolutions in the generally accepted sense of the word are rare. Most important from the point of view of international relations is the fact that major revolutions are not, it seems, autonomous and insulated from outside forces. Quite the reverse: the course of each of them has been fundamentally affected by external intervention. What constitutes intervention is certainly disputable. Marxist theorists have already called attention to the pressures of the world economy on the internal social order of individual states as a factor in revolution, and following the dependency theorists, some have seen the operation of the capitalist system itself as a sort of 'economic intervention'. Here, however, I have wished to show that more traditional interpretations of intervention, military and diplomatic, have their own very special role to play. Undoubtedly, both forms of intervention may on occasion be prompted by the desire to safeguard existing investment or trade links. If so, however, the political consequences of doing so cannot be escaped.

For, thirdly, it is in restraining the impulse to intervention that a state finds its best chance of avoiding revolution in a friendly state, and even of securing its long-term objectives at the cost of some minor and temporary inconveniences. Intervention does not stop revolutions, it helps cause them. It does not even matter much whether or not the threat to a 'revolutionary' state is real, what matters is that it is perceived as such. Hence, President Carter's attempt to rescue the Iranian hostages, although in no way a danger to the survival of the Islamic revolutionary regime, was seen as such purely because of the power of the state mounting the operation. The result was the further radicalisation of the revolution at a moment at which its internal contradictions might well have begun to set it on the course to political disintegration.

For a foreign policymaker to conduct relations with a revolutionary regime bent on making life difficult for him

and so getting its own way, is never easy. It requires three
things in all states: self-restraint, knowledge of the situation,
and a certain amount of luck. But in the case of liberal
democratic states a fourth factor must also be present: the
support of the electorate. To achieve this for a policy of self-
restraint is a very difficult task indeed. It is seldom a popular
policy in itself, and it is always possible that populistic demo-
gogues will force the hand of the government with their
strident calls for violent solutions that will solve nothing
and make matters worse. Nor can a government reasonably
expect its supporters to be as well informed as it is itself.
Hence, it is the duty of every citizen to try to understand
that with the greater knowledge that is now available to us,
compared with what was known in 1793 or 1918, we can
indeed be confident that such a strategy is right. Indeed, we
can go further and say that it is not only in our self-interests,
but also in that of the world community as a whole, to which
in the long term our own individual interests are all linked.
The principal conclusion of this book, hence, is that citizens
should in future expect and demand of their governments
a policy of enlightened self-restraint.

In drawing this conclusion I do not, of course, ignore the
evidence that in many cases revolutionary movements in
individual countries have sought to ensure their survival in
the world by propagating their ideas abroad and even by
using subversion to try to secure governments friendly to
themselves. What I have done is to point out that the actual
overthrow of governments is a very different matter. Propaganda in itself cannot harm a government if the internal
political and social conditions are not favourable for its
reception. Indeed, the free exchange of ideas is a sign of
vigorous social health. Appeals to would-be nationalist
minorities, even, need not be too much of a problem for the
stability of the country as a whole, always provided that the
government avoids the temptation of being stampeded into
a posture of repression. Even during the French Revolution,
it was not French ideas but French armies that installed the
governments.

Dealing with a revolutionary government, therefore, is
something that can be done with safety as well as confidence

if the government that is carrying out the negotiation is confident in the support of its own people. It will be much easier for it to keep that support if it is more widely realised that it is in the interests of even revolutionary states to keep to the forms and rules of international diplomacy. To them it may well seem outdated, a system that they did not devise and which they would prefer to destroy rather than to join. At one time this might have been possible. Today, though, the system has extended world-wide, and even those nations that once most strongly objected to it as a relic of the past, such as the United States, France and the Soviet Union, now find that they must accept it, or have no alternative to the consequences of all-out confrontation. As their cases show very clearly, there is nothing in the international sphere that a revolutionary state wants to have as badly as it wants recognition, and in the present-day world all sides have an interest in being the first to extend it and to gain the 'friendship' of the new regime. Wise diplomats, therefore, will not try to drive hard bargains at this point, but instead, by judicious concessions to secure a state of affairs in which the new government sees clearly that it has much more to gain than to lose from negotiation. One need look no further than the history of the IMF loans in the 1970s to realise that as long as the negotiating process can be kept going, even the most powerful countries can be led to find that they are making concessions that they would previously have thought unimaginable, and discovering their interests as better preserved in the process.

For social science teaches above all that all historical analogies have their limitations outside which they are no longer valid. In the twentieth century nationalism has certainly been powerful, but in a form different from that of the nineteenth century, and with the ending of decolonisation the forces it has generated must logically be subsiding. The use of internal military repression on a massive scale has certainly brought quiet to some countries for a brief period at a time, but here too populations have changed in their awareness owing to the spread of ideas and information, and the path of peace by ignorance is no longer a viable option, even if it were not in any case morally abhorrent. Most dangerous of all, in a world divided by superpower confrontation and overshadowed by the threat of nuclear extinction for the whole of humanity, would be for any substantial state to think that it could simply opt out of the world. The temptation in such circumstances for one or other of the superpowers to be drawn into a regional confrontation has repeatedly been demonstrated—in Cuba, in Ethiopia and in the Gulf War, as well as for two political generations in the Middle East. It would be much better for them, and much safer for the world, if their leaders were to come to realise that neither revolution nor counter-revolution need affect their own vital interests unless they choose to have them do so. What they can change, in short, is both their perception of threat and their degree of confidence in what is really vital.

They will, of course, do even better if they look at the world for the opportunities it presents, rather than the threats they fear; for the chance to improve what they have inherited, rather than the ability to destroy what others may wish to keep.

Bibliography

Adorno, T. W., Frenkel Brunswik, Else, Levinson, Daniel J., and Sanford, R. Nevitt (1964), *The Authoritarian Personality*, New York, John Wiley.

Afrifa, Colonel A. A. (1966), *The Ghana Coup 24th February 1966*, London, Frank Cass.

Arnell, Lars, and Nygren, Birgitta (1980), *The Developing Countries and the World Economic Order*, London, Frances Pinter and Methuen.

Bell, J. Bowyer (1976), *On Revolt; Strategies of National Liberation*, Cambridge, Mass., Harvard University Press.

Billington, James H. (1980), *Fire in the Minds of Men; Origins of the Revolutionary Faith*, New York, Basic Books.

Black, Cyril E., and Thornton, Thomas P. (1964), *Communism and Revolution, the Strategic Uses of Political Violence*, Princeton, Princeton University Press.

Brier, Alan (1982), 'Revolution as a form of political succession', unpublished paper for Planning Session on Political Succession, ECPR Joint Sessions of Workshops, Freiburg, 1982.

Brier, Alan, and Calvert, Peter (1975), 'Revolution in the 1960s', *Political Studies*, 32, No. 1, March 1975, pp. 1–11.

Brinton, Crane (1952), *The Anatomy of Revolution*, New York, Vintage Books.

Bull, Hedley (1977), *The Anarchical Society*, London, Macmillan.

Calvert, Peter (1967), 'Revolution: the politics of violence', *Political Studies*, 15, No. 1, February 1967, p. 1.

Calvert, Peter (1970a), *Revolution (Key Concepts in Political Science)*, London, Pall Mall and Macmillan.

Calvert, Peter (1970b), *A Study of Revolution*, Oxford, Clarendon Press.

Calvert, Peter (1976), 'On attaining sovereignty', in Anthony Smith (ed.), *Nationalist Movements*, London, Macmillan.

Canetti, Elias (1973), *Crowds and Power*, Harmondsworth, Penguin Books.

Cardoso, Fernando Enrique, and Faletto, Enzo (1979), *Dependency and Development in Latin America*, Berkeley, University of California Press.

Carr, Raymond (1966), *Spain, 1808-1939*, Oxford, Clarendon Press.

Chakotin, Serge (1940), *The Rape of the Masses: the Psychology of Totalitarian Political Propaganda*, London, Routledge.

Clutterbuck, Richard (1973), *Protest and the Urban Guerrilla*, London, Cassell.

Crozier, Brian (1960), *The Rebels: A Study of Post-War Insurrections*, London, Chatto & Windus.

Dahrendorf, Ralf (1961), 'Über einige Probleme der sociologistischen Theorie der Revolution', *Archives Européenes de Sociologie*, 2, No. 1, 1961, p. 153.

Davies, James C. (1962), 'Toward a Theory of Revolution', *American Sociological Review*, 43, No. 1, February 1962, pp. 5–19.

Debray, Régis (1965), 'Latin America: the Long March', *New Left Review*, 33, September–October 1965, p. 17.

Debray, Régis (1969), *Revolution in the Revolution?*, London, Penguin Books.

Diederich, Bernard (1978), *Trujillo, the Death of the Goat*, London, Bodley Head.

Drummond, S. H. (1979), *British Involvement in Indonesia, 1945–1950*, unpublished Ph.D. dissertation, University of Southampton, 1979.

Duff, Ernest A., and McCamant, John F. (1976), *Violence and Repression in Latin America*, New York, The Free Press.

Durkheim, Emile (1965), *The Division of Labor in Society*, trs. George Simpson, New York, The Free Press.

Eckstein, Harry (ed.) (1964), *Internal War*, New York, The Free Press.

Eisenstadt, S. N. (1978), *Revolution and the Transformation of Societies*, New York, The Free Press.

Erikson, Erik H. (1968), *Identity: Youth and Crisis*, New York, W. W. Norton.

Eysenck, H. J. (1963), *The Psychology of Politics*, London, Routledge.

Falk, Richard A. (1962), 'Revolutionary nations and the quality of international legal order', in Morton A. Kaplan (ed.), *The Revolution in World Politics*, New York, John Wiley.

Fals Borda, Orlando (1965), 'Violence and the break-up of tradition in Colombia', in Claudio Veliz (ed.), *Obstacles to Change in Latin America*, New York, Oxford University Press.

Feinberg, Richard E. (1983), *The Intemperate Zone; The Third World Challenge to U.S. Foreign Policy*, New York, W. W. Norton.

Feit, Edward (1973), *Armed Bureaucrats*, Boston, Houghton Mifflin.

Finer, Samuel E. (1962), *The Man on Horseback*, London, Pall Mall.

Frank, André Gunder (1969), *Latin America; Underdevelopment or Revolution*, New York, Monthly Review Press.

Frank, André Gunder (1978), *Dependent Accumulation and Underdevelopment*, London, Macmillan.

Frankel, Joseph (1979), *International Relations in a Changing World*, Oxford, Oxford University Press.

Freud, Sigmund (1965), *Group Psychology and the Analysis of the Ego*, trs. James Strachey, New York, Bantam Books.

Fromm, Erich (1960), *The Fear of Freedom*, London, Routledge.

Gamson, William A. (1975), *The Strategy of Social Protest*, Homewood, Ill., The Dorsey Press.

García Marquez, Gabriel (1978), *One Hundred Years of Solitude*, London, Pan Books.

Giap, Vo Nguyen (1965), *People's War, People's Army*, New York, Praeger.

Gibb, C. A. (ed.) (1969), *Leadership*, Harmondsworth, Penguin Books.

Goldenberg, Boris (1965), *The Cuban Revolution and Latin America*, London, Allen & Unwin.

González, Luis J., and Sánchez Salazar, Gustavo A. (1969), *The Great Rebel; Che Guevara in Bolivia*, New York, Grove Press.

Goodspeed, D. J. (1962), *The Conspirators; A Study of the Coup d'Etat*, London, Macmillan.

Gott, Richard (1970), *Guerrilla Movements in Latin America*, London, Nelson.

Greig, Ian (1973), *Subversion: Propaganda, Agitation and the Spread of People's War*, London, Tom Stacey.

Gross, Feliks (1958), *The Seizure of Political Power in a Century of Revolutions*, New York, Philosophical Library.

Guevara, Ernesto Che (1967), *Guerrilla Warfare*, New York and London, Monthly Review Press.

Guevara, Ernesto Che (1968a), *The Complete Bolivian Diaries of Che Guevara and Other Captured Documents*, (ed.) and intro., Daniel James, New York, Stein & Day.

Guevara, Ernesto Che (1968b), *Reminiscences of the Cuban Revolutionary War*, trs. Victoria Ortiz, London, Allen & Unwin and Monthly Review Press.

Gurr, Ted Robert (1970), *Why Men Rebel*, Princeton, Princeton University Press.

Haas, Ernst B. (1965), *Beyond the Nation State: Functionalism and International Organization*, Stanford, Stanford University Press.

Haley, P. E. (1982), *Congress and the Fall of South Vietnam and Cambodia*, New Jersey, Fairleigh Dickinson University Press.

Hall, Stuart, and Jefferson, Tony (eds) (1977), *Resistance Through Rituals; Youth Subcultures in Postwar Britain*, London, Hutchinson.

Harris, Richard L. (1970), *Death of a Revolutionary; Che Guevara's Last Mission*, New York, W. W. Norton.

Havens, Murray Clark, Leiden, Carl, and Schmitt, Karl M. (1970), *The Politics of Assassination*, Englewood Cliffs, NJ, Prentice-Hall.

Herz, J. (1959), *International Politics in the Nuclear Age*, New York, Columbia University Press.

Hibbert, Christopher (1958), *King Mob: the Story of Lord George Gordon and the Riots of 1780*, London, Longmans.

Hobsbawm, E. J. (1972), *Bandits*, Harmondsworth, Penguin Books.

Hobson, John Atkinson (1968), *Imperialism: a Study*, London, Allen & Unwin.

Hoffer, Eric (1951), *The True Believer, Thoughts on the Nature of Mass Movements*, New York, Harper.

Holsti, K. J. (1967), *International Politics, a Framework for Analysis*, Englewood Cliffs, NJ, Prentice-Hall.

Horowitz, Irving Louis, comp. (1967), *The Rise and Fall of Project Camelot: Studies in the Relationship Between Social Science and Practical Politics*, Cambridge, Mass., The MIT Press.

Hughes, John (1968), *The End of Sukarno: a Coup that Misfired: a Purge that Ran Wild*, London, Angus & Robertson.

Hyams, Edward (1975), *Terrorists and Terrorism*, London, Dent.

James, William (1907), *Pragmatism*, London, Longmans.

Johnson, Chalmers (1964), *Revolution and the Social System*, Stanford, The Hoover Institution on War, Revolution and Peace.

Johnson, Haynes (1965), *The Bay of Pigs: the Invasion of Cuba by Brigade 2506*, London, Hutchinson.

Jung, Carl Gustav (1933), *Psychology of the Unconscious: a Study of the Transformations and Symbolisms of the Libido*, London, Kegan Paul.

Kirkham, James F., Levy, Sheldon G., and Crotty, William (1970), *Assassination and Political Violence*, New York, New York Times Books.

Labrousse, Alain (1970), *The Tupamaros*, Harmondsworth, Penguin Books.

Lasswell, Harold D. (1960), *Psychopathology and Politics*, New York, Viking Press.

Lawrence, Thomas Edward (1926), *The Seven Pillars of Wisdom*, London, M. Pike with H. J. Hodgson.

Le Bon, Gustave (1960), *The Crowd: a Study of the Popular Mind*, intro. Robert K. Merton, New York, Viking Press.

Leiden, Carl, and Schmitt, Karl M. (1968), *The Politics of Violence; Revolution in the Modern World*, Englewood Cliffs, NJ, Prentice-Hall.

Lenin, Vladimir Ilyich (1967), *Selected Works*, Moscow, Foreign Languages Publishing House, 3 vols.

Little, Richard (1975), *Intervention; External Involvement in Civil Wars*, London, Martin Robertson.

Lorenz, Konrad (1966), *On Aggression*, London, Methuen.

Luttwak, Edward (1968), *Coup d'Etat, a Practical Handbook*, London, Allen Lane, The Penguin Press.

McDonald, Joan (1965), *Rousseau and the French Revolution 1762–1791*, London, University of London, The Athlone Press.

McDougall, W. (1920), *The Group Mind*, Cambridge, Cambridge University Press.

McMichael, R. Daniel and Paulus, John D. (eds) (1983), *Western Hemisphere Stability—the Latin American Connection*, Pittsburgh, World Affairs Council of Pittsburgh 19th World Affairs Forum.

Machiavelli, Niccolò (1950), *The Prince and The Discourses*, New York, Random House.

Malaparte, Curzio (1932), *Coup d'Etat, the Technique of Revolution*, trs. Sylvia Saunders, New York, E. P. Dutton.

Marighela, Carlos (1971), *For the Liberation of Brazil*, Harmondsworth, Penguin Books.

Martí, José (1968), *The America of José Martí: Selected Writings*, trs. Juan de Onis, New York, Funk & Wagnalls.

Martin, Everett Dean (1920), *The Behaviour of Crowds, a Psychological Study*, New York and London, Putnam.

Marx, Karl, and Engels, Frederick (1962), *Selected Works*, Moscow, Foreign Languages Publishing House, 2 vols.

Meisel, James H. (1965), *Pareto and Mosca*, Englewood Cliffs, NJ, Prentice-Hall.

Mercier Vega, Luis (1969), *Guerrillas in Latin America; the Techniques of the Counter-State*, London, Pall Mall.

Michels, Robert (1959), *Political Parties: a Sociological Study of the Oligarchical Tendencies of Modern Democracy*, New York, Dover Publications.

Miller, Norman, and Aya, Roderick (eds) (1971), *National Liberation: Revolution in the Third World*, New York, The Free Press.

Minogue, Kenneth (1969), *Nationalism*, London, Methuen.

Monge Alfaro, Carlos (1966), *Historia de Costa Rica*, San Jose, Imprenta Trejos Hnos.

Moore, Barrington, Jr. (1969), *Social Origins of Dictatorship and Democracy; Lord and Peasant in the Making of the Modern World*, London, Peregrine Books.

Morris, Desmond (1969), *The Naked Ape*, New York, Dell.

Nasution, Abdul Haris (1965), *Fundamentals of Guerrilla Warfare*, facsimile edn., intro. Otto Heilbrunner, New York, Praeger.

Neuberg, A. (1970), *Armed Insurrection*, London, NLB.

Nicolson, Harold (1963), *Diplomacy*, London, Oxford University Press, 3rd edn.

Nkrumah, Kwame (1965), *Neocolonialism, the Last State of Imperialism*, New York, International Publishers.

Oppenheim, Lassa Francis Lawrence (1952), *International Law: a Treatise*, ed. H. Lauterpacht, London, Longmans, 7th edn.

Oppenheimer, Martin (1970), *Urban Guerrilla*, Harmondsworth, Penguin Books.

Osanka, Franklin Mark (ed.) (1962), *Modern Guerrilla Warfare: Fighting Communist Guerrilla Movements, 1941–1961*, New York, The Free Press.

Paret, Peter, and Shy, John W. (1962), *Guerrillas in the 1960s*, New York, Praeger, rev. edn.

Pearce, Jenny (1981), *Under the Eagle: U.S. Intervention in Central America*, London, Latin American Bureau.

Perls, F. S. (1969), *Ego, Hunger and Aggression; the Beginning of Gestalt Therapy*, New York, Vintage Books.

Pettee, George Sylvester (1938), *The Process of Revolution*, New York, Harper & Brothers.

Pustay, John W. (1965), *Counterinsurgency Warfare*, New York, The Free Press.

Putney, Snell, and Putney, Gail J. (1964), *The Adjusted American; Normal Neuroses in the Individual and Society*, New York, Harper & Row.

Richardson, Lewis (1960), *Statistics of Deadly Quarrels*, London, Stevens & Sons.

Rosenau, James N. (ed.) (1964), *International Aspects of Civil Strife*, Princeton, Princeton University Press.

Rudé, George (1964), *The Crowd in History: A Study of Popular Disturbances in France and England, 730–1848*, New York, John Wiley.

Russett, Bruce M. (1964), *World Handbook of Political and Social Indicators*, New Haven, Yale University Press.

Sansom, Robert L. (1970), *The Economics of Insurgency in the Mekong Delta of Vietnam*, Cambridge, Mass., The MIT Press.

Satow, Sir Ernest (1957), *A Guide to Diplomatic Practice*, London, Longmans.

Schram, Stuart R. (ed.) (1963), *The Political Thought of Mao Tse-tung*, New York, Praeger.

Seton-Watson, Hugh (1977), *Nations and States: an Inquiry into the Origins of Nations and the Politics of Nationalism*, London, Methuen.

Short, Anthony (1974), *The Communist Insurrection in Malaya, 1948–1960*, London, Frederick Miller.

Skocpol, Theda (1979), *States and Social Revolutions: a Comparative Analysis of France, Russia and China*, Cambridge, Cambridge University Press.

Smelser, Neil J. (1962), *Theory of Collective Behavior*, London, Routledge.

Smith, Anthony D. (ed.) (1976), *Nationalist Movements*, London, Macmillan.

Sorel, Georges (1950), *Reflection on Violence*, trs. T. E. Hulme and J. Roth, intro. Edward A. Shils, Glencoe, Ill., The Free Press.

Sorokin, Pitrim Aleksandrovitch (1937), *Social and Cultural Dynamics III; Fluctuation of Social Relationships, War and Revolution*, New York, American Book Company.

Spanier, John W. (1967), *World Politics in an Age of Revolution*, New York, Praeger.

Stanford Central America Action Network (1983), *Revolution in Central America*, Boulder, Colo., Westview Press.

Stevens, Evelyn P. (1974), *Protest and Response in Mexico*, Cambridge, Mass., The MIT Press.

Stodgill, R. M. (1948), 'Personal Factors Associated with Leadership; A Survey of the Literature', *Journal of Psychology*, 34, No. 1, 1948, p. 35.

Stokes, William S. (1959), *Latin American Politics*, New York, Thomas Y. Crowell.

Sunday Times Insight Team (1975), *Insight on Portugal; the Year of the Captains*, London, Andre Deutsch.

Taber, Robert (1965), *The War of the Flea: a Study of Guerrilla Warfare Theory and Practise*, New York, Lyle & Stuart.

Talmon, Jacob L. (1961), *The Origins of Totalitarian Democracy*, London, Mercury Books.

Thayer, Charles W. (1963), *Guerrilla*, London, Michael Joseph.

Thompson, James W., and Padover, Saul K. (1963), *Secret Diplomacy, Espionage and Cryptography, 1500–1815*, New York, Ungar.

Thompson, Robert (1970), *Revolutionary War in World Strategy, 1945–1969*, New York, Taplinger.

Tiger, Lionel (1969), *Men in Groups*, London, Nelson.

Trotsky, Leon (1966), *History of the Russian Revolution to Brest-Litovsk*, London, Gollancz.

Trotter, William Finlayson (1953), *Instincts of the Herd in Peace and War*, London, Oxford University Press.

Truong Chinh, pseud. of Dang Xuan Khu, *Primer for Revolt, the Communist Takeover in Viet-Nam: A Facsimile Edition of The August Revolution and The Resistance will Win*, intro. and notes, Bernard B. Fall, New York, Praeger.

Vagts, Alfred (1959), *A History of Militarism, Civilian and Military*, London, Hollis & Carter.

Vittachi, Tarzie (1967), *The Fall of Sukarno*, London, Mayflower-Dell.

Wilkie, James W., and Wilkie, Edna (1970), *The Mexican Revolution: Federal Expenditure and Social Change since 1910*, Berkeley, University of California Press.

Wilkinson, Paul (1974), *Political Terrorism*, London, Macmillan.

Wilkinson, Paul (1978), *Terrorism and the Liberal State*, London, Macmillan.

Wise, David, and Ross, Thomas B. (1964), *The Invisible Government*, New York, Random House.

Wolf, Eric (1970), *Peasant Wars of the Twentieth Century*, New York, Harper & Row.

Wolfenstein, E. Victor (1967), *The Revolutionary Personality: Lenin, Trotsky, Gandhi*, Princeton, Princeton University Press.

Wolfgang, M., and Ferracuti, F. (1964), *The Subculture of Violence*, London, Tavistock Press.

Wright, Quincy (1965), *A Study of War*, Chicago, University of Chicago Press, 2nd edn.

Yablonsky, Lewis (1962), *The Violent Gang*, New York, Macmillan.

Ydígoras Fuentes, Miguel (1963), *My War with Communism, as Told to Mario Rosenthal*, Englewood Cliffs, NJ, Prentice-Hall.

Zartman, I. William (1966), *International Relations in the New Africa*, Englewood Cliffs, NJ, Prentice-Hall.

Index